Fifty years ago Tom Hughes was a noteworthy practitioner of the British art of after-dinner speaking. Typical audience reactions at the time included:

"Unlike Queen Victoria, I was amused" (Zbigniew Brzezinski). "Delicious" (Robert Amory). "Urbane, witty, graceful—toastmanship supreme" (Richard Nolte). "A dazzling virtuoso performance" (Milton Crane). "The whole place was abuzz" (James Gardner). "Superb with wit and flavor" (Edgar Shannon). "The kind of irony we need more of" (Marquis Childs). 'I enjoyed every line" (John Gardner). "Most amused, paradoxical as it may seem" (Harry McPherson). "Vintage Hughes" (Benjamin Welles). "A masterpiece" (Leonard Meeker). "Absolutely glorious"(Anthony Lewis).

OXFORD AFTER DINNER

THOMAS L. HUGHES

iUniverse, Inc.
Bloomington

Oxford After Dinner

Cover photo courtesy of The Rhodes Trust

Photograph of author courtesy of Chad Evans Wyatt

iUniverse books may be ordered through booksellers or by contacting:

iUniverse
1663 Liberty Drive
Bloomington, IN 47403
www.iuniverse.com
1-800-Authors (1-800-288-4677)

ISBN: 978-1-4502-9201-6 (sc)
ISBN: 978-1-4502-9202-3 (ebook)

Printed in the United States of America

iUniverse rev. date: 4/15/2011

FORWARD

My husband, Thomas Hughes, had many contacts with Britain even while growing up in the 1930s and 1940s in southern Minnesota four thousand miles away. There were prewar visits from Welsh relatives and wartime correspondence with aging cousins and young contemporaries in England. While a teenager he had also met several Rhodes Scholars who had already taken their places in American public life.

In 1944 as a Carleton College freshman, Tom was elected the second national president of Student Federalists, a group that advocated a postwar federal union of the United States and Britain. During his undergraduate years he also majored in international relations with a minor in English history and literature. Thus by interest and inclination he was prepared to take full advantage of a Rhodes Scholarship, which came his way upon his graduation from Carleton in 1947.

In both high school and college Tom had also won national awards in debate and oratory. After his arrival at Oxford he quickly joined the Oxford Union debating society where he frequently spoke. Perhaps, as a result, he was invited by the BBC to represent President Truman in its nationally televised debate the night before the American presidential election of 1948. During his time at Oxford Tom also wrote articles for Minnesota newspapers about his life in postwar Britain.

Over the ensuing decades while working on Capitol Hill, in the State Department, or at the Carnegie Endowment for International Peace, Tom often went back to Britain as a visitor. In 1969-70 he served as the minister and deputy chief of mission of the American Embassy in London. Later as president of the Carnegie Endowment he also returned to Oxford to speak, as when he introduced German Chancellor Willy Brandt at the dinner following the presentation of Brandt's honorary degree in 1980.

Over the years Tom recaptured his British experiences in lighthearted after-dinner speeches in Washington, New York, London, and elsewhere. The celebrated Oxford professor, Sir Isaiah Berlin, was among those in Tom's audience at the 1965 Oxford-Cambridge dinner in Washington. After reading another such speech seven years later, Berlin wrote him from Oxford:

"Dear Tom,

"I enjoyed your remarks enormously, particularly the pungent asides. I do envy your capacity for making thoroughly delightful, entertaining, and indeed informative after-dinner orations. I wish I could! Total inability to do this is one of the fatal impediments in my present administrative career at Wolfson College.

"Someone ought to write a thesis about the importance of after-dinner speeches in the English-speaking world, for it is only in that world that it matters at all. But it matters a good deal at times. Sometimes it leads to bliss and glory, and sometimes to immeasurable wastes of shame.

Yours sincerely,

Isaiah Berlin

July 10, 1972"

Here are seven of Tom's after-dinner speeches that typically evoked such high-level fan mail. They range over three decades and they all reflect Tom's graceful relationship with the English language. Moreover, like his many serious speeches and articles, they are infused with wit and detachment.

As period pieces, they should be read in context. They frequently contain allusions to major events at the time of their delivery. These "Oxford After Dinner" speeches also reflect the hubris of the meritocracy of the 1960s and 1970s, the gradual fading in later years of the Anglo-American "Special Relationship," and, naturally, the nostalgia of aging audiences for their golden youth.

In 1999, half a century after he himself went down from Oxford, Tom was asked to reminisce by the new Rhodes Scholars who were about to leave for England. Those remarks appear first below because they retrospectively set the context. The other six after-dinner speeches follow in consecutive order:

1. "At Oxford Only Yesterday" at the Rhodes Scholars Bon Voyage Panel, the Cosmos Club, Washington, DC, September 26, 1999.

2. "Oxford's Revenge" at the Oxford-Cambridge Boat Race Dinner, the National Press Club, Washington, DC, March 31, 1965.

3. "A Post Report at Thanksgiving" at the American Society in London Dinner, Dorchester Hotel, London, England, November 27, 1969.

4. "Leaves from the Journal of Our Life in Imagine" at the Annual Oxford-Cambridge Dinner, Shoreham Hotel, Washington DC, April 11, 1972.

5. "The Efficient Secret of Oxford" at the American Rhodes Scholars 75th Anniversary Dinner, University Club, New York, NY, September 25, 1978.

6. "Tearing or Mending?" at the American Rhodes Scholars Reunion, Georgetown University, Washington, DC, June 12, 1993.

7. "An Anglo-American Update" at the Class of 1947 Rhodes Scholars Reunion, Williams College, Williamstown, MA, June 22, 1996.

Jane Casey Hughes

February 2011

A NOTE FOR THE READER

By Thomas L. Hughes

Near the close of the twentieth century, as one of the first post-World War II Rhodes Scholars, I spoke informally to the annual group of Americans who were about to leave for Oxford to take up their scholarships. I was asked to reminisce about our experience of Oxford fifty years earlier. My impromptu remarks that day may help set the context for the six Oxford after-dinner speeches that follow.

AT OXFORD ONLY YESTERDAY
Rhodes Scholars Bon Voyage Panel
Cosmos Club, Washington, DC
September 26, 1999

The first full contingent of postwar Rhodes Scholars set sail for England in the old Queen Elizabeth, from New York to Southampton, the first week of October, 1947. Compared to our prewar predecessors, we were a significantly different group, going to a distinctly different Oxford and a drastically different England. The ship itself had only just been reconverted for passenger use from its wartime troop service.

Many of us were war veterans and thus some years older than our prewar predecessors had been when they came up. Some of us had been prisoners of war or were among the walking wounded. Many of us were married, and in attempting to make the adjustment to wedded Rhodes Scholars, the warden of Rhodes House tried to make the young wives feel welcome by stressing their good luck. He told them that probably nothing would be more important in their lives than the fact that they were married to Rhodes men. Clearly the really new Rhodes Scholars--the non-males, non-WASPS, and non-whites--were still way over the future horizon.

Oxford itself was full of anomalies. True, its serene time warp was still there. In that sense it was one of the last outposts of prewar Britain. It had escaped wartime bombing, according to rumor, because Hitler had chosen it for his future capital after the conquest. But Oxford, even then, was regarded as painfully overcrowded. The traffic was oppressive. Rooms in college were usually shared.

Compared to the "Brideshead Revisited" years of the prewar university, Oxford was a far more serious and sober place. There was now a ten-year age gap among the British students. Mustached veterans with six years of war service found themselves classmates of boys just up from school—boys who still qualified for the monthly banana quota given by ration boards to those under seventeen.

All of us carried our slim rations of butter, jam, and sugar across the quad to and from breakfast every morning. The Union Society suspended its evening meals in order to provide modest ones at noon. Some of us at Balliol used to frequent the nearby British Restaurant where, for a shilling, a cheap government subsidized lunch provided relief from the ghastly one at college. Scouts still lit the coal fires in our rooms and thawed out the ice in our washbasins that had frozen overnight.

An alarming number of students actually worked hard. A weekly total of forty hours of private reading, not counting lectures, tutorials, seminars, and societies, was not unusual. The legendary highjinks of earlier years were largely missing, although we did join in the all-night celebrations of the royal wedding of Elizabeth and Philip in November 1947.

We also got off to a fast start. I remember my very first evening at Balliol attending a brilliant off-the-cuff after dinner discourse by Lord Lindsay, the master of the college. It was based on a book he was then reading called "A Farewell to European History," written by Max Weber's brother Alfred.

The next morning I went to the Sheldonian to sample a lecture by A.J.P. Taylor. He began speaking while walking up the long aisle to the lectern, and as he passed by he was saying: "You young people would do well to remember that a primary objective of the great powers before the first World War was to make sure that Italy was on the other side when the war began."

That same evening Harold Laski held forth at the Union rhapsodizing about his recent visit to Moscow. "I wish you could have seen the gleam in Stalin's eye when he said goodbye to me that night at the Kremlin." I thought, I am going to like this place.

Oxford received a steady parade of celebrities. The prime minister, members of the Cabinet, and hosts of ordinary MPs visited regularly. Americans including Secretary of State George Marshall and former first lady Eleanor Roosevelt came to collect honorary degrees.

Lady Astor invited us down to visit Cliveden. Her country house had, of course, been the center of the appeasement set in the 1930s, but we were too polite to bring that up. She was a Virginian and told us that she never knew how proud she was of her background until she saw "Gone With the Wind."

Lady Astor had also just been to see Stalin, but her approach differed from Laski's. "I asked Stalin," she said, "'when are you going to end the Czarist regime?' And the translator fainted."

Some of us signed up for a political theory seminar with Professor G. D. H. Cole. He had just written "The Intelligent Woman's Guide to the Postwar World." At the first seminar he looked over the group and said, "I see there are Americans here. Let me ask them a simple question: do you believe in political science?"

A couple of my unsuspecting colleagues raised their hands indicating that they did. "Out! Out! Outside of America there is no such thing as political science. You may leave. There is nothing scientific about it. In my seminars we only deal with political theory. Those who accept these ground-rules may remain."

Some of us had debated in college in the US and so we signed up to speak at the Oxford Union. Once there, we had to make a speedy adjustment. We learned that an epigram easily outweighed the encyclopedia. The US national debate subject the previous year had been a heavy one, "Resolved: that a federal world government should be established." By contrast my first two debates at the Oxford Union were typical. The first was "Resolved: that this house thinks Columbus went too far."

The second was "Resolved: that this house deplores the fact that while woman first induced man to eat, he took to drinking all alone."

Our classmate Kenneth Tynan delivered his swan song speech at the Union when the topic was "Resolved: that this house wants to have it both ways." Tynan took the negative because the topic implied that there were only two ways to have it.

The last years of the 1940s were of course historic ones: the Nuremberg trials, the Marshall Plan, the founding of NATO, the communist coup in Czechoslovakia, the creation of Israel, and the independence of India. The latter in many ways symbolized the enormous reduction in the postwar British role and the psychological ambivalence felt by many in Britain about the consequent American ascendancy.

World War II had been the greatest Anglo-American collaborative enterprise in history. Many Oxford dons and students alike had experienced the so-called "Special Relationship" in a dangerous, exhilarating wartime setting. We Americans benefited, of course, from the consequent gratitude and the reflected camaraderie. But it was gratitude tempered by envy and a certain resentment. Sometimes this was expressed in strong terms: "You are the Herrenvolk now." The British were left with their overseas investments depleted, a huge balance-of-payments problem, a worn out industrial machine, a war-wearied population, and a big decline in world status.

Meanwhile at home, America was consumed with anti-Communism, the Hiss case, and its first postwar presidential election. I remember sitting in a tutorial with Lord Lindsay at Balliol in November 1948. We were interrupted by his wife, who styled herself Mrs. Lindsay because, as a socialist, she objected to the title. She said, "It's the BBC calling." When her husband rose to answer the phone, she surprised us both. "No, Sandy, it's not for you. It's for Mr. Hughes."

The BBC's search for someone to go on television to speak for President Truman the night before the US election had come all the way around to me. "We had no trouble locating a supporter for Governor Dewey and also one for Henry Wallace, but we have tried everywhere without success to find a supporter of President Truman.

Someone told us that there was a student at Oxford named Hughes who might be willing to speak for Mr. Truman." I quickly made myself available.

The next day a chauffeur drove me to London and the Alexandra Palace for nationwide TV, then in its rudimentary beginnings. We were wined and dined and then put on the screen. When it was all over and I was back at Balliol, someone told me that I had begun my remarks with a scarcely ringing endorsement. Apparently I had said that the American people were about to choose between two of the least seductive personalities in American public life, but that given the choice, I was for Truman.

Above all, of course, we lived in Labour Britain. Clement Attlee was prime minister. Both in British political life and in Oxford intellectual life democratic socialism and the welfare state were terms of high aspiration, not opprobrium. The contrast with America's free-booting capitalism was rubbed in regularly. The class struggle, national health, public housing, and guaranteed incomes—these were the subjects of national and undergraduate debate.

I even joined the Labour Party and went with thirty Oxford socialists for a weekend retreat at Lord Faringdon's Berkshire estate. A hereditary peer and a Labour sympathizer, his lordship was an expert in colonial administration and was a prominent defender of the government in the House of Lords. For three days we roamed around his eighteenth century house, set amid acres of trees and fountains, formal gardens, statuary, outdoor theater, swimming pool, et cetera.

Our committee sessions were held under rows of van Dykes and Reynoldses. We slept in four-poster beds dreaming of the classless society. I thought to myself: this is not the way the Farmer-Labor party in my native Minnesota demonstrated the fervor of its class consciousness. A visit to the annual Labour party conference, however, at the grimy, kitschy, seaside playground of Blackpool, soon restored my sense of proportion.

Of course, we also amused ourselves. We were surrounded by good conversation and good music. Even those not engaged in college sports, cycled around the beautiful Oxford countryside. London, Stratford, Wimbledon, and Blenheim were near at hand.

The splendid Rhodes hospitality scheme took me for wonderful weeks to Argyle, Devon, Kilkenny, and elsewhere. Most of us headed for Italy during the first spring vacation.

I had the good luck to have a girlfriend who was in Paris for her junior year abroad. One bright morning we were scheduled to meet on the train at London's Waterloo station for a trip to Wales. As the train began to depart with me aboard, I suddenly noticed that she was still on the platform. In jumping off the moving train with my baggage, I superficially skinned my knee on the platform, thereby promptly inaugurating the British National Health Service. It was the opening day, and an ambulance, white-coated doctors, telegenic nurses, cameras and news photographers were quickly on hand. The pictures in the papers the next day were captioned: "National Health treats American as first patient at Waterloo."

All in all, we scholars in the late 1940s found, as you will too, that Oxford gave us the freest and most stimulating years of our young lives.

Good luck and Godspeed.

OXFORD'S REVENGE
Toastmaster's Remarks
Oxford-Cambridge Boat Race Dinner
National Press Club
Washington, DC, March 31, 1965.

THE GRACE: Ladies and Gentlemen, pray silence and rise for The Grace, which will be said by the Right Reverend Angus Dun, the Bishop Emeritus of Washington.

THE LOYAL TOASTS: I call upon the Charge d'Affaires of the British Embassy, Mr. Michael Stewart of Trinity College, Cambridge, to propose the toast to the President.

I call upon the Majority Leader of the House of Representatives, Mr. Carl Albert of St. Peter's, Oxford, to propose the toast to the Queen.

THE HEAD TABLE: Your Excellencies, Bishop Dun, Mr. Attorney General, Members of the Congress and fellow members of Oxford and Cambridge Universities. It gives me great pleasure on behalf of your dinner committee to welcome you to the 19th annual Boat Race Dinner. I am told that our attendance is nearly 250 which makes this not only the largest such dinner ever held in Washington, but very possibly the largest gathering of members of the two universities ever jointly assembled in this country.

Distinctions among distinguished people are always untenable, usually unwise, and in the case of these dinners, not customary. I would, therefore, like only to mention those head table guests who come tonight from overseas --either as ambassadors or as visitors from the universities themselves. They include:

The Ambassador of Canada from Pembroke, Oxford.

The Ambassador of Greece from Christ Church.

The Ambassador of Israel from Wadham.

The Ambassador of Jamaica from Wadham.

The Ambassador of Malawi from King's.

The former Master of University College, Oxford, and Mrs. Goodhart.

The Chichele Professor of Social and Political Theory, Sir Isaiah Berlin, from All Souls.

Mr. Robert Farquharson, Fellow of Churchill College, Cambridge.

Apologies for Absence have been received from:

The Secretary of State of St. John's, Oxford,

Mr. Justice Harlan of Balliol,

Mr. Justice Stewart of Trinity, Cambridge.

Mr. Justice White of Hertford.

Senator Fulbright of Pembroke, Oxford.

The Honorable Dean Acheson of both Oxford and Cambridge.

I think you will understand when I say that there is another dinner tonight at 1600 Pennsylvania Avenue being given by Southwest Texas State Teachers College's most eminent alumnus, and that some of our most regretted absences are attributable to that.

Oxford's Revenge: On the River

A decent supply of port has been made available to you for the many toasts you will be called upon to drink. Your Committee voted for port despite news from Oxford that the Franks Commission, now investigating all facets of university life, has heard testimony under oath that far less port is being drunk these days than ever before.

I suggest that it is possible to make your port last if you will consume it in the proper proportions. Employing Pentagon language for a moment, if you will engage in a deliberate and graduated response to the provocations which will be put to you--if your response is, indeed, measured and fitting --then your supply of port may last the evening. Should you nevertheless exhaust your port supply, I beseech you to follow this simple proscription: leave your neighbors alone. If you take their port, they may not stand idly by with folded arms. They may administer a sound rebuff.

Confronting that ultimate scenario, you may actually want to forget the port altogether, and escalate to the more adventuresome substitutes offered--for a price-- by your waiter. Or, you may fall back on a less tasty, but more assured, alternative. As Castro reportedly said when he shut off the pipes at Guantanamo: "Water taken in moderation cannot hurt anybody."

And after all, water taken in moderation is what brings us together again tonight. It flows, in moderation, in the Isis and the Cam. And it flows past all the historic milestones of the championship course on the Thames: from Putney Bridge to Fulham, Leander Club, Craven Steps, Ranelagh, the Mile Post, the Crabtree, Harrod's, Hammersmith Bridge, the Doves, Eyot, Chiswick Steps, and the Reach—along Duke's Meadows, Barnes Stanbury, White Hart, The Ship—in short all the four and a quarter miles from Putney to Mortlake.

And what Oxonian and Cantabrigian has not been immoderately moved by the dramas that have been enacted upon that classic course? Scenes from the past 110 races flood through our memories, including the dead heat of 1877 and the ignominy of 1912, when both boats sank. A two-boat finish is the rule, however, and the score is now 61 for Cambridge to 48 for Oxford with one tie. However, when we recall that Cambridge founded its boat club in 1827, and that Oxford did not follow until 1839, Cambridge can be said to have a twelve year advantage which can never really be righted. Indeed that almost precisely makes up for the thirteen point difference in the totals.

I am sure you were as offended as I by that article in the Washington Post last Sunday which began impertinently: "Ahh, the Oxford-Cambridge Boat Race. All the Right People get excited about it. Nobody remembers who won last year." How wrong the author was. Remember? How could we forget? For Cambridge, a runaway win. For Oxford, a humiliating loss. Here is the account of the Sunday Times' own rowing correspondent, writing from Mortlake, fresh from viewing the 1964 finish:

"Cambridge won the toss, and as always, chose the Surrey station. For over half the way Cambridge were too far ahead to see closely, but it was at least clear that they rowed with integrity. So did Oxford in form, but after the start the sense of urgency departed and did not return until it was too late. Even so, unlike most beaten crews, Oxford looked fresh at the finish. If a single reason may be accepted for the result it is there.

"Cambridge came to Putney patently inferior except in muscle power. But their will to win, coupled with the magic of their final coaching, improved them so much that with the nose of their boat in front, it was impossible for them to lose. So they won. But Oxford should not forget that they lost the 110th boat race and can have no complaint about it."

Do I hear cheers from Cambridge? Let them cheer. The rest is Oxford. Indeed all that has followed, and all that will follow tonight, may as well be titled "Oxford's Revenge."

When your committee notified me of my assignment tonight, I assumed that it must have something to do with my daytime assignment as Director of Intelligence and Research in the Department of State. So, for starters, I am prepared to offer you certain intelligence reports. Their sources fall naturally into one of those categories that we familiarly use inside the government: a usually reliable source, an unusually reliable source, a usually unreliable source, or, more rarely, an unusually unreliable source. In any case it all adds up to intelligence, to be contradicted only by events as they actually occur and are reported in the press.

My first report is to reassure you that not everyone took General de Gaulle seriously when he proclaimed that "…the reasons for subordination to America are disappearing one by one." For example, this year the President of the Oxford Boat Club defied this advice from Paris and put four Yale men in the Oxford boat.

To date, the results have been spectacular. On March 19, the Oxford boat beat the all-time record from Putney to Mortlake (P to M) by rowing the full course in 17 minutes, 37 seconds, taking seven intermediate records en route. Enthusiasm and confidence are still mounting at Oxford over this fortuitous bonanza from Yale.

According to the Oxford Boat Club President, "Trippe, Spencer, Howell, and Fink have been chosen because of their ability, not their origin." As the Duke of Wellington said after reviewing some new recruits: "I don't know what effect they will have on the enemy, but they frighten me to death."

Mind you, some excessively academic observers, who are probably unsympathetic to exercise in general, have complained about the makeup of this year's Oxford boat. "With one or two exceptions," said the Warden of Wadham recently, "colleges expect their rowers of boats to be reasonably literate." Now this may indeed explain why there is no one from Wadham in the boat this year, and only one each from Lincoln and the House. But there are two from Keble, and five from St. Edmund Hall. It all adds up to a kind of Multilateral Force composed of Yale, Keble, and Teddy Hall.

That MLF allusion perhaps sheds light on another report that the Admiralty has not been above a certain interest in the outcome for Oxford this year. Its representatives on the Thames Water Commission are reputedly watching Oxford's practice races with more than their usual attention.

One report in particular simply cannot be dismissed out of hand. It suggests that the success or failure of this Anglo-American Multilateral Force on the Oxford boat may not be unrelated to Her Majesty's Government's eventual decision on the larger question of nuclear management. You will recall the emotions which had been stirred, and the opinions which had been ventilated, when we last heard of the MLF, prior to the time when American interest in the matter suddenly went beneath the surface itself. All this happened last Michaelmas term, just as the new government came to power in Whitehall and boat race training began.

At that time Field Marshall Montgomery was saying: "I hold the view that anybody who thinks that Britain should not be a nuclear power must be crackers—indeed, absolute crackers."

But a Labour Lord was more doubtful: "I can only look at this project as a kind of academic Suez, equally nostalgic, equally impractical, and equally embarrassing to get out of."

The sportsman's journal, "The Camper," had editorialized: "The big weakness of Western Europe is the lack of fish and chip shops."

But now in the Oxford boat, you have mixed manning on a surface ship with no Western Europeans and no kitchen at all. A stalking horse? A contrived precursor? A laboratory experiment to be unveiled as HMG's long awaited proposal for an allied nuclear force? Who knows? At any rate the boat race will be over, and the results will be in, in good time, for the most thorough re-evaluation and processing—long before we pass through the Bank Holiday, the grouse season, the German elections, and all the other prerequisites for renewing the multilateral discussion.

This line of speculation is partially supported by yet another intelligence report that Kosygin would have liked to attend the boat race, were he to be in England on Saturday. Already a Soviet naval attache has been seen with binoculars on the towpath in the Reach. But the Admiralty has reacted with its customary aplomb. "Not only the Russians survey other peoples' exercises," says the Commander-in-Chief of the Home Fleet. "I look on it as a healthy method of mutual naval education."

Against this array of double blue talent, Yale and Oxford mixed, what can be said of Cambridge this year? There are no Americans on the Cambridge crew, and only one Australian. Yet ten days ago, just a day after Oxford beat the old record, Cambridge beat it also, rowing only ten seconds slower than Oxford over the full distance. So Oxford has been saved from complacency, and Cambridge is greatly encouraged.

Under these tightening odds, the press has become unusually active in introducing new variables to justify continued betting on opposing outcomes. "It is difficult to control the direction of the wind on a Saturday afternoon in April," according to the Daily Telegraph. The weather forecasts in the Express are notably more cheerful than those in its rival newspapers.

As tension mounts, the Right People are reportedly being joined by the Wrong People. Mods and Rockers are said to be turning out for the race, waving light blue or dark blue, depending on where their fathers or mothers went. Or on whether they prefer light blue or dark blue. Just the other night, a brawl of Rockers was attracting attention in a back street in Clacton when a shout was heard above the fray: "No, not if you was to kill me, I wouldn't be Cimebridge."

One MP has suggested: "It would surely be far better for the Mods and Rockers, and for the rowing community at large, if, instead of breaking up Fulham and Hammersmith, and places like that, they all stayed home from the boat race and read a little light pornography instead."

While the experts are still betting on Oxford, and dark blue blood is pulsating heavily with dark blue throats ready to cheer, and while the Admiralty and the Russians keep their eyes on the mixed-manned Oxford boat, something can yet happen to spoil Oxford's revenge. Caution instructs us to expect surprise. We should not exclude even a last minute French entry in the Cambridge boat. As General de Gaulle has said: "If everything were settled in advance, it would not be interesting."

Oxford's Revenge: On Shore

If Oxford's revenge on the river must remain in doubt until Saturday, Oxford's revenge on shore has taken shape beyond dispute. To put matters in a proper perspective, in the last quarter century, five of Britain's six Prime Ministers have been Oxonians, which, if you will pardon my saying so, is as it should be. As we consider some of their characteristics as men, rather than politicians, we shall quickly discover living proof both of the poverty of ideology and of Oxford's lifelong impact.

Which Oxonians present do not recognize, in the following vignettes, certain distinctive elements of the Oxford heritage too precious for denial? –As when Prime Minister Attlee, despite appearances to the contrary, said: "It is a great mistake to make government too dull." Or when an MP complained to Prime Minister Eden in the Commons' question period: "The more time the Prime Minister has, the less information he gives us."

Or when Prime Minister Macmillan confessed at Oxford six years ago: "I rather enjoy patronage. I take a lot of trouble over it. At least it makes all those years of reading Trollope worthwhile."

Of course it was Macmillan also who said: "Mr. Attlee had three old Etonians in his cabinet. I have six. Things are twice as good under the Conservatives."

Or when the following was disclosed about Sir Alec Douglas-Home in last autumn's campaign by his stalwart colleague, Rab Butler: "I will give away the Prime Minister's secret. Whenever things became most tense, Sir Alex would go off on his own for half an hour and arrange a vast bowl of flowers."

Or when Prime Minister Wilson now says in Commons: "I am probably one of the few Prime Ministers who cleans his own shoes." To which a back bencher replies: "We do not pay our Prime Minister to clean his own shoes."

Of course the Prime Ministers from Oxford have also competed through the years to see who could do the most for Oxford. As a don-politician, the new Prime Minister, Mr. Wilson, was expected to be especially susceptible to his Oxford ties. Oxford high tables confidently reverberated with predictions that they would provide the same kind of support for the new government that White's Club did for the old. The Hampstead Set was said to have ties even to Cambridge.

The hearts of holders of Firsts in Economics from both Universities beat especially high. Was not the new Prime Minister himself a First in Economics? Was he not once described as the "cleverest man in Oxford?" Never mind that many of the supplicants themselves had described him in less favorable terms over the years. They allowed their names to be put forward without shame.

Thus once more, last autumn, the aspirants for Cabinet appointments, Oxford and Cambridge alike, held their breath. As Tory ministers were bumped by their Socialist successors, the reverberations extended into the Congregation at Oxford and Regent House at Cambridge. And no wonder. Consider the record in all its stark simplicity:

Prime Minister and First Lord of the Treasury: Christ Church, Oxford, bumped by University College, Oxford.

Lord Chancellor: Magdalen, Oxford, bumped by Magdalen, Oxford.

Secretary of State for Foreign Affairs: Pembroke, Cambridge, bumped by Christ Church and St. John's, Oxford.

Secretary of State for Defense: Royal Military Academy, Woolwich, bumped by Balliol, Oxford.

Secretary of State for the Home Department: Balliol Oxford, bumped by Balliol. Oxford.

Secretary of State for the Colonies: Magdalen, Oxford, bumped by Balliol, Oxford.

President of the Board of Trade: "Balliol, Oxford, bumped by New College, Oxford.

Lord Privy Seal: Magdalen, Cambridge, bumped by New College, Oxford.

Secretary of State for Education and Science: Christ Church, Oxford, bumped by Trinity, Oxford.

Minister of Housing and local Government: Magdalen, Oxford, bumped by New College, Oxford.

These Cabinet bumpings read more like Eights Week at Oxford than like anything from Putney to Mortlake. Balliol once more is head of the river, and Cambridge, poor thing, has been bumped completely out of the Cabinet. Should we not indeed speak of Oxford's Revenge? Eleven seats in this boat for Oxford. None, none at all, for Cambridge.

"The ship's afloat, brother, and there's no reverse gear" said Mr. George Brown in December. "The risk is that one will tend to get caught up in the sheer exhilaration of making decisions, and in the desire to make them fast, forgetting the point about getting them right." But had Mr. Brown been an Oxford man, he would have known that all this new crew had to do would be to return, every now and then, to their university moorings—back to Oxford—where it has always been clear what is right and what is wrong.

Unexpectedly, toward the end of January, there was one last chance for Cambridge. Old ambitions again stirred uneasily. Was a Cambridge man once more in the lists for Foreign Secretary? We were all on tenterhooks that day, even in the State Department.

Early that morning, I had given Secretary Rusk the racing ticket as we saw it, and I took him word of the selection of his new counterpart that afternoon. He received the news with a knowing smile, for the new Foreign Secretary was more than Oxford. He was St. Johns, Oxford, a tie which now binds the Foreign Office and the State Department and binds them at the top. It is that same perspective which once prompted Mr. Rusk to say to no one in particular: "I would not, if I were you, worry about the British."

(Introduction of Howard K. Smith for the Toast to the Universities.)

We have been speaking of Oxford's Revenge—on the river, in the Cabinet, and in the conduct of foreign affairs. But there is one thing that really tires Foreign Secretaries-- even those blessed with a patience earned under the Italian delicacy of St. John's arcades, or in the pools of ilex shade beyond her Archery Lawn-- and that is being questioned by the press. Journalists, I am told, divide diplomats into two classes: those who know but don't tell, and those who tell but don't know. But the matter is further complicated by the repressed desire of many journalists to be diplomats, and of many diplomats to be journalists.

Benjamin Jowett advised nineteenth century Balliol diplomats to "Never apologize; never explain." Advice like that, when followed today, makes life desperately complicated for hardworking television reporters like our next speaker. Such diplomatic behavior is said to lead reporters to an over-concentration on bread and circuses, and a neglect of the things that matter most.

Thus BBC-TV anticipates upwards of ten million boat race viewers on Saturday, most of whom have already placed their bets on Oxford with their favorite bookies. Faced with this prospect, the editor of BBC-TV news complained publicly last week: "A lot of people are interested in the future of Europe as well as the boat race." To which the right reply is obvious—that it is far better to be worked up about unimportant issues than not to be worked up at all.

One might have thought that it would be a challenge for the ancient universities to come to terms with television. But not at all. The difference in values has proved to be more apparent than meets the eye. The two cultures overlap more and more with the development of commercial television.

The famous debate of 1952 has receded beyond recall. Gone are the days when Lord Reith was protesting that "…somebody introduced smallpox, bubonic plague, and the Black Death into England. Somebody," he said," is minded now to introduce sponsored broadcasting." At the time, the reply came quickly from none other than Mr. John

Profumo, who, speaking in favor of commercials, made his historic statement: " We are not, after all, a nation of intellectuals."

The commercial channel soon discovered Oxbridge, and they with fervor returned the compliment. "Television seems to need face-to-face communicators," said Dr. Mark Abrams, a specialist in market research. "That is the special skill which Oxbridge provides: people who know when to be flippant and when to be serious, who can say the right things about Wimbledon and Glyndebourne." The Prime Minister himself is personally sensitive to these nuances. "My speeches are all different," he said the other day, "and they are all my own work, too, if you will excuse that brief commercial."

And so, with dons crowding the trains to London to joust with one another on the BBC, what could be more fitting than that the toast to the universities tonight should be proposed by one of our most notable television commentators, one who has had his own memorable experiences with sponsors and news management, one whose popularity continues to testify to the proposition that one man with ideas counts for as much as a hundred who merely have interests. I call upon Howard K. Smith of Merton, Oxford, to propose the toast to the Universities.

(Introduction of Attorney General Nicholas Katzenbach
for the Response for the Universities.)

Eighteen years ago, fortified by Yale like this year's Oxford crew, your next speaker was discussing with his wife, Lydia, his intention to do some graduate work in England. They had heard of England's three great educational institutions—Oxford, Cambridge, and Balliol. They talked it over and concluded that Cambridge was all very well, but Balliol happened to be situated at Oxford.

Over seven centuries Balliol had produced a proud hatchery of kings, prime ministers, archbishops, cardinals, viceroys, statesmen, jurists, scientists, philosophers and poets. For half a century, Jowett had been looking down from his Platonic heaven, smiling his contentment as all this stream of effortless superiority continued to exert itself.

"Better at Balliol with nothing than at Trinity with an Exhibition," Archbishop Temple told his son.

Hilaire Belloc wrote a poem "To the Balliol men still in Africa." And if we are to believe Lord Samuel, they are still there: "Where there are two D. Phils. in a developing country, one is Head of State and the other is in exile. Both probably went to Balliol."

Today the new white-brick University of Sussex, outside Brighton, presided over by its Balliol Vice Chancellor, reportedly aspires to be known as "Balliol By the Sea."

Balliol itself has resumed its lead in the final honour schools. Twenty percent of Balliol men are regularly winning Firsts again. Balliol is once more primus inter pares in the Cabinet. Balliol has elected its first confessedly Marxist master. It's the same the whole world over. Floreat domus de Balliolo--roughly translated boola boola Balliol.

This process of Balliolization has spread, like the process of Texanization in Washington. When these two trends intersect, the result is likely to be formidable. It was. It gave Balliol its first United States Attorney General.

To those Washingtonians familiar with President Johnson's instinct for the telephone, a new and deeper meaning has been given to Mathew XXI-13: "Many are called, but few are chosen." During his five months' vigil as Acting Attorney General, your next speaker was often called. As the President himself has remarked, "He got to know me a little."

Today Nick's greatest fan is Mary McGrory of the Washington Star. She has written of him as "a large, calm man, bright-eyed, heavy footed, who speaks in a pleasant baritone which congressmen find forceful and soothing. He has a reassuring manner. He lacks the alienating aura of power and glamour of his predecessor as well as the latter's quivering contentiousness. He occasionally ventures a light remark, but it is never too clever. He has the calming presence of a mastiff, responsive and not obtrusive."

Miss McGrory continues: "When pickets sat outside his office door, Katzenbach was in his shirtsleeves. He had a silver mug of coffee before him. Then Katzenbach got up and swung away from his desk. 'I've got to do a little thinking,' he said, and moved heavily into another office. Outside the pickets shouted 'Freedom!'"

Once more it is time to say: "Well rowed, Balliol." I call upon the Attorney General of the United States to give the response for the Universities.

(Introduction of Congressman John Brademas for the Toast to the Ladies.)

At a recent debate in the Oxford Union, the question was: "Resolved: that the American House of Representatives should aspire to be more like the House of Lords than the House of Commons, but that it doesn't care." The motion was adopted 61 ayes, 59 nays.

The arguments were the predictable ones. The first speaker for the motion scored the following points: We in England are fortunate to have inherited the House of Lords, an institution which we would never have had the intelligence to create. Left to our own devices, we might have found ourselves encumbered by something like the Americans' own House of Representatives, never mention their Senate."

The first speaker against the motion defended the House of Commons. It is called together, he noted, at very frequent intervals to give it an opportunity of hearing the latest legislation and allowing the members to indulge in cheers, sighs, groans, votes, and other expressions of vitality. After having cheered as much as is good for them, they go back to the lunchrooms and go on eating, until they are needed again.

The speaker added that it is an entire exaggeration to say that the House of Commons no longer has a real share in the government of England. Indeed anybody connected with the government values the House in a high degree. One of London's leading newspaper proprietors himself says that he has always felt that if he has the House of Commons on his side, he has a very valuable ally.

The second speaker for the motion referred to President Johnson and the Vietnam crisis, drawing from it some morals for the behavior of elected officials generally. He suggested that American Congressmen might emulate the House of Lords at a time of crisis. He quoted the stanza from Iolanthe:

> "When Wellington thrashed Bonaparte
>
> As every child can tell,
>
> The House of Peers throughout the War
>
> Did nothing in particular,
>
> And did it very well."

The final speaker against the motion argued that American legislators could benefit from the House of Commons' pioneering role in legislation. Today the House of Representatives suddenly discovers new truths, which were commonplace in the Commons decades ago. Thus, fashioners of the Great Society should consider the prior British experience. Any amount of raw new thinking could be avoided in this way.

To illustrate the point, the speaker mentioned that questions have now been put in Parliament asking whether a doctor's duties under Britain's national health program include answering emergency night calls for contraceptives. Admitting that he had a personal interest in the answer, the speaker added that we would all find the supplementary questions even more stimulating than the original one. Who claims that the Congressional Record has nothing to learn from Hansard?

According to Lady Violet Bonham-Carter, the Tories hold their party together by not allowing their left wing to see what their right wing is doing. Your next speaker likewise manages to keep one wing in BNC and the other wing in South Bend. He knows that inconclusive discussions at Oxford are nevertheless inadequate training for political success in the Great Society.

Hence he has tried to make up the difference by joining the Masons, Ahepa, the Eagles, the Moose, the Methodists, the National Conference of Christians and Jews, and the American Legion. Your committee thought it would do its bit by offering him this opportunity to appeal to the women's vote. I call upon the Representative from Indiana, the Honorable John Brademas of Brasenose, Oxford, to propose the toast to the Ladies.

(Introduction of Mrs. Martin-Trigona for the Response from the Ladies.)

The strength of the ladies has never really been tested on the river. This is only the second year in history for the Oxford-Cambridge women's boat race. I am sorry to say that Cambridge has won both times. This year was a disaster for the Oxford ladies' boat. Their number 2 caught a crab right at the start, and the women lost their rhythm. Cambridge went on to win by four lengths.

This inexperience on the river is perhaps one reason why ladies in ascendancy occasionally make deplorably bad judgments just after they taste newly acquired power. Consider the principal of Somerville who has been testifying before the Franks Commission. She allowed herself to take on the clergy in a singularly maladroit appeal: "Divinity has eight professors at Oxford," she said, "while biology, a field that I know, has only four. Divinity is not the most lively field of discovery at the present moment, while exciting things are happening in biology. At Oxford our ideas about what is important are just about seven hundred years out of date."

Had Dame Janet had experience on the river, I dare say she would never have made so innocent an attack on the heart of the Oxford way of life. There is an ancient and unshakeable alliance between the cloth and the river, from the days of John the Baptist straight through a century of boat race history. Did she not know that all but three of today's bishops in the Church of England went to Oxbridge, and that two of the others went to Trinity, Dublin? Litchfield, Gloucester and Chester all rowed in their university boat. Had not Portsmouth been a Rugger blue, he too might have been a celebrity on the river. As Sydney Smith said a century ago, "What our bishops like best in their clergy is a dropping -down -deadness of manner." Where else could the clergy best learn that, if not in Oxbridge boats?

The clergy in Oxford have been quick to retaliate for Dame Janet's ill-advised remarks. Stung by her accusations that divinity is not as exciting as biology, they have suddenly given a spurt of attention to both. Stirred into action by her challenge, they have competed with one another to demonstrate divinity's liveliness on the great issues of the day. By enlisting with excitement in the great university sex debate, they are fast undermining Oxford's reputation for logical thought and exposition. Controversy abounds in Oxford pulpits over the rustication of an American undergraduate for having a woman in his room in the early hours.

Thus we have heard from the broadminded pulpit of St. Martin's; "A steady love affair, though illicit, is reasonably safe from the national point of view."

And from the subtle pulpit of St. Aldate's: "The weak who know how to play on their weakness are strong. This is the secret of women and the developing countries."

And from the popular pulpit of St. Peter-in-the-East: "It has to be admitted that we English have sex on the brain, which is a very unsatisfactory place to have it."

And from the Dean of St. Edmund Hall, home of so many of this year's Oxford crew: "Fornication, we know, is nothing like the sin to end all sins, but it is a sin. And to pretend otherwise will do nobody any good."

Unlike Oxford divines who heedlessly embarked on this boiling controversy, our final speaker this evening is worldly wise. She has attended seven colleges and universities, all of them coeducational. She has an Oxford B. Litt. She speaks Greek. Her biography says that she was "one of the first… American girls to go to the Middle East" in World War II. Since then she has traveled widely from Luxemburg to the Ascension Island to Suez. She knows all about rhetoric and Francis Bacon. Allow me to call upon Helen Martin-Trigona of St. Hilda's, Oxford, who will give the Response for the Ladies.

It only remains for me to thank the other speakers and your committee for all the effort that has gone into this event. It has been a cooperative endeavor, reminding us all of those two ancient stone cities with their quadrangles, cloisters, spires, damp staircases, and punts—reminding us too that despite occasional appearances to the contrary, America and Britain, like Oxford and Cambridge, unavoidably will find themselves swept along in the same current, rowing in the same international mainstream.

That is why I venture to say that all of the non-Englishmen present will give the benefit of the doubt to former President Eisenhower. He said not long ago in that inimitable style of his which we miss so much: "Britain is still a very fine nation to have on our side." Thank you and good night.

A POST REPORT AT THANKSGIVING
The American Society in London Dinner
Dorchester Hotel, London, England,
November 27, 1969

Mr. Chairman, Mr. Ambassador, my Lords, Ladies and Gentlemen: Successive announcements about this dinner have been read by me with growing trepidation. First, I received a printed handbill advertising your evening's entertainment as "one of the best cabaret acts you will ever see." At the bottom of the handbill in large red letters were the words: "Plus Two Surprises!" Dignity at once led me to discount any possible connection with the cabaret act. So I concluded that I was one of the two surprises, and I set about speculating over the identity of the second.

Earlier this week I had concluded that the other surprise would be John Lennon without his MBE. Now over the years, as we all know, attitudes have fluctuated on the relative merits of orders in this country. Lord Melbourne himself used to say that what he liked about the Order of the Garter was that there was no damn Merit about it. John Lennon of Bag has obviously been thinking similar thoughts about his MBE. Most of you will have read the letter he sent to the Queen last Tuesday, when he returned his insignia to Buckingham Palace:

"Your Majesty:

I am returning this MBE in protest against Britain's involvement in the Nigerian-Biafran thing, against our support of America in Vietnam, and because (my) record 'Cold Turkey' has slipped down in the charts. With love,

John Lennon"

Yoko has said that she and John have had the "same vibrations" on this issue. However, his Aunt Mimi told the press yesterday that she, Mimi, had been "profoundly upset and had tossed and turned all night trying to fathom out what made John do this awful thing."

John now says that he is upset that his Aunt Mimi is upset, but that he had really been thinking about returning the MBE for some time. Suddenly the thought had come to him, "Now is the time."

As I tried to put myself in the Lennons' place, I could just see them lying there on Monday, thinking about Thanksgiving three days away, and figuring that at the rate "Cold Turkey" was slipping—from 16 to 17 to 18—it would be right off the charts altogether by Thursday. Hence John might as well come over here to the Dorchester for hot turkey instead. The timing all made sense.

But as it turns out, John is not purged of his medal after all. A Palace spokesman is quoted as saying that it will be kept in a drawer for him, and if at any time John wants it back, he may have it. A spokesman for the Prime Minister has explained that while John has returned his insignia, he will not be able to divest himself of the order. "He still remains an MBE."

So the surprise is on John, not on us, and he probably would not want to come here under the circumstances. There is, of course, a considerable difference between "Cold Turkey" slipping down in the charts and hot turkey slipping down at the Dorchester. But I am afraid that this is one on that short list of life's experiences which the Lennons are determined to forego. And I am left still speculating about the surprises your chairman has promised.

Meanwhile, a second and different advance copy of tonight's program reached me from the American Society. Along with it came an exhortatory letter, which was at pains to point out what was really required. It instructed me that the Society has held these dinners almost every year since 1895, and there has been what the letter called "a short—invariably witty—talk by a distinguished guest like Sir Winston Churchill, the Duke of Windsor, Viscount Montgomery, Earl Mountbatten, General Marshall" and other invariably witty men.

Naturally, I had known of some of their wit. Sir Winston, for example, not only said but did many witty things. Some of his wittier deeds have even been commemorated in bronze, like many of his grander and soberer ones. I have in mind the plaque on the guest room door in President Roosevelt's house at Hyde Park, New York, which reads: "The following important people have slept here. The King and Queen of England, President and Madam so-and-so of France, Winston Churchill and the Grand Duchess Charlotte of Luxembourg."

And I can readily recall witty things associated with Field Marshal Viscount Montgomery. Not only is he adept at selling paintings at the right price to willing buyer.* But also one thinks of Montgomery's well known description of El Alamein— "There were two contestants in that battle—Rommel on his side and I on mine." And one remembers his view of Whitehall—that you have to be physically fit in order to be mentally fit, and that very few people at Whitehall are physically fit.

When I went on to consider your other previous speakers, like Lord Mountbatten, the Duke of Windsor, and General Marshall, I said to myself: one can hardly deny that the American Society in London has had a rollicking good time for itself at these events over the years.

Indeed it was rather like Prime Minister Wilson's description of the Labour Party a few years ago at a time of lesser party dissension: "I have always felt that the Labour Party—don't misunderstand me when I say it—has got something in common with an old stagecoach. I do not mean it is out of date, but if it is rattling along at a rare

---

* Ambassador Annenberg had purchased General Eisenhower's portrait of Montgomery's at Sotheby's the day before.

old speed, most of the passengers will be so exhilarated, and some so seasick, that they won't start arguing."

Yet there is not much for the American Society in London to argue about anyway when you come to think of it. You have all undertaken the Pilgrims' journey in reverse, which is how you happen to be in London. As the latest participant in that West-to-East pilgrimage, I propose to bring you up to date by recounting a few of my own recent migratory experiences as I prepared for and undertook the trans-Atlantic crossing. With your indulgence, that is what I shall now set out to do.

One of our obscure Presidents of the last century, Millard Fillmore, discovered that he was running for the Presidency when he was informed by a servant girl who got the news at the local telegraph office. She knocked on Fillmore's door and said: "I have the honor to inform you that you have been nominated for the Presidency of the United States, ridiculous as that may seem."

The phrase recurred one day last spring in Washington when I heard Secretary of State Rogers say: "Ridiculous as it may seem, we want you to go to London as the new Minister in the Embassy there." When I expressed suitable surprise, he added: "I hear that you have been to Oxford and all that." I failed to protest that my mother, like Max Beerbohm, used to say that I had been a modest, good humored boy, but it was Oxford that had made me insufferable.

When it gradually became bruited about in London, in the circles that brood about such things, that I, like my distinguished predecessor, had gone to Balliol, there must have been many here who simply sighed that life is just one Balliol man after another.

Under these circumstances, who is going to contradict former Prime Minister Macmillan's prescription for getting ahead in Britain:"Don't jaw, don't intrigue. Get on with the job you're asked to do. It helps," Macmillan added, "if you are a Balliol man."

As last spring wore on into summer, and my wife and I began to make our plans to move, I asked Secretary Rogers if he had any special instructions to help prepare us for London. One day in June he handed me a copy of the guidelines which a predecessor of his of fifty years ago, Bainbridge Colby, gave to all foreign service officers as final admonitions for their tour abroad. "If they were good enough for Secretary Colby," Mr. Rogers said, "they're good enough for me." The instructions read:

"Be guarded in your choice of associates. Never permit society to interfere with your official duties. Live modestly and always within your means. Do not loan money. Keep out of debt. Be American first, last, and all the time."

The last four of these instructions had a particular poignancy for me, when I remembered that a Scottish great-grandfather of mine could have saved himself a lot of trouble if he had kept both his patriotism and finances in better order. Born to be a poet, he never quite came to recognize that if you want to write poetry, you have to earn your living some other way. In an unsuccessful search for the latter, he eventually settled on a windswept farm in Minnesota, having meanwhile taken a calamitous route from Scotland to Canada, Panama, California, and Iowa.

In 1885, during one of his periodic crises when his poetry got the better of his farming, he wrote to Queen Victoria. He told her that he had just sworn allegiance to President Cleveland, but that he didn't really mean it. Meanwhile would she be so kind as to send him five guineas to tide him and his family of twelve through the harsh Midwestern winter? And if he could please receive the funds by Thanksgiving, so much the better.

There is no record of a reply from Windsor Castle.

In all likelihood the royal recipient on this, as on other occasions, was not amused. One wonders whether she or her loyal supplicant in Minnesota would have been more shaken by Prince Philip's recent explanation of the royal family's cash predicament—by the early encouraging headlines reading "Funds Roll in for the Queen," followed by the later dispiriting return of the gifts to the senders whom Buckingham Palace describes as "ordinary people"—Chelsea pensioners, office girls, professional people, and the like. It is obviously just as hard today to give cash to the Queen as to return an MBE.

But let me return to my own story. By July the Administrative Officer of the European Bureau in the State Department had presented me with a copy of the Department's latest "Post Report" entitled: "City—London, Country—England." If I now read you some excerpts from it, you will see what a comprehensive and eye-opening introduction it was to the life that lay before us.

"This is the official 'Post Report,' prepared at the post. Any other information you receive covering the facts contained in this report is to be regarded as unofficial information. An assignment to London may surely be welcomed, for life in this great metropolis presents no particular hazards, and only a few restrictions…

"Travel En Route to Post. Those arriving very late at night or very early in the morning probably will not be met by an American member of the Embassy staff, but usually arrangements can be made to have them met by a car and chauffeur recognizable by the American eagle emblem on his cap and buttons.

"London buses are excellent, comparing favorably with those in use in the United States. Taxicabs are of a special construction, and plentiful, except when it rains… English automobiles can be purchased in the United Kingdom. However, this action is not recommended in view of the U. S. program to save gold.

"Orientation and General Description of Post. Identification and Location: The American Embassy, usually referred to by the British as the United States Embassy, is located on Grosvenor Square, a ten minute walk from the center of the famous Mayfair area. London (itself) is located on the River Thames about forty miles from the river mouth, and almost 3,875 miles from New York City. It is in the same relative position as Labrador.

"The imperial gallon is 1/5th larger than the American gallon… There are 20 shillings to the pound…During the 19th century, Britain led an empire on which the sun never set. Today Britain is more nearly an island dependent on its own efforts…There are signs that out-dated methods are changing as both management and labor see the advantages of modernization.

"Life at the Post. (While) London suffers from no problems of mildew or insect and vermin infestation, houses are not as well heated as in the United States. 'Central heating' does not approximate the average American idea of 'steam heat.' Most English people are quite happy in a house where the thermometer registers around 65 degrees. This situation is best met by dressing as the English do…Fires are occasionally comfortable during the summer months.

"Transportation and Communication. There is no postal censorship in England, and one uses normal postal channels for letter mail. Airmail takes 1 to 2 days from New York and parcel post 2 to 3 weeks. Shipments should contain no tobacco, liquids, firearms, or explosives (see footnote).

"Footnote on firearms. It is not recommended that firearms which require registration and certificates be shipped to the United Kingdom. Air rifles, air pistols, smooth bore shotguns with barrels of 20 inches or more, and antique firearms incapable of being fired, are the only firearms not requiring registration and certification. Gas pistols, presently being manufactured in Germany, will not be authorized entry into the United Kingdom and are liable for confiscation regardless of the owner's status. Individuals with diplomatic status are not excused from the registering procedure; they should be prepared to estimate for the police the number of rounds of ammunition they will require during their tour of duty.

"Recreation and Social Activities. London offers a variety of newspapers and several influential weeklies, but no real news magazines are published in Britain. Time and Newsweek are readily available at almost every newsstand in London, however, in addition to Continental publications of every type.

"Improvers of the breed find familiar pleasure at world-famous Epsom Downs, Ascot, and half-a-dozen other nearby tracks.

"Due to the identity of language and other similarities, Americans in London do not form a 'colony' as they invariably do in non-English speaking countries. For this reason it is not usual for them to gather together as a group except at their respective clubs and at special social events." (Like meetings of the American Society in London.)

By August we were fully briefed and nearly ready to leave, when additional vistas, unmentioned in the "Post Report" vividly opened before us. One of my Oxford contemporaries, Ken Tynan, the inventor of "Oh Calcutta," suddenly arrived on Broadway proclaiming that England was now "an open, socialist, sexually expanding society, where everything can be fun." People began to ask me how eight years in the State Department could have prepared me for so many-sided an assignment.

Speculating on the full dimensions of our move, I momentarily thought of some earlier days on Capitol Hill, and of Senator Flanders of Vermont telling of the trauma of his first election to the Senate. On the day of his departure for Washington, the citizens of Springfield, Vermont, gathered around a haymow to bid the Senator-elect goodbye. A spokesman mounted the platform and addressed him as follows: "And now, Senator, as you leave the familiar rolling hills of our Vermont countryside to take up your tasks in the nation's capital, you leave us in the certain knowledge that in moving from Springfield to Washington you will be raising the moral level of both communities."

I was unsure precisely how this diagnosis would apply to our own move. But I did in fact find, as soon as I arrived in London—and I assure you that this is as true as the trade figures—an envelope marked "Personal for Mr. Hughes—to be opened on arrival." Inside was a letter which read:

"Mr. Hughes:

"As I have been searching for my father for lo these many years, I have taken the chance of leaving you this note. If it so happens that I am mistaken once again, please excuse me for this small arrest of your attention. If I am not mistaken, I may be reached aboard the yacht Paulina. She is berthed in Heybridge Basis, Maldon, Essex. Sincerely, Lawrence P. Hughes."

I was perplexed over how to handle this touching appeal, and there were the customary divided counsels inside the Embassy. Just then an erroneous but helpful account of my arrival appeared in one of the London evening papers. Among other things, it mistakenly credited me with having a "Bachelor of Theology" degree. Someone had penned a note across it which read: "Just what a minister should have." I seized the opportunity and sent the clipping off to Lawrence at the yacht Paulina, confident that that would answer his question. It must have done so, as I have not heard from him again.

Speaking of ministers, especially at Thanksgiving-time, and to make up for my errant Scottish great-grandfather, I should at least mention another ancestor of mine who was a genuine, ferocious-looking New England pilgrim. I have a letter signed by him in 1660, in his capacity as Secretary of the Massachusetts Bay Colony. In it he records the determination of the General Court that "all places and people be supplied of an able and faithful minister" and that therefore orders were to be issued concerning "the maintenance of the ministers and the purging of towns from such ministers as shall be found vicious in theire living or perniciously heterodox in theire doctrine." Note the implication that ministers may be heterodox as long as they are not perniciously so.

Incidentally if you wonder what it is like to a be a minister, think what it is like to be a minister's wife. Once Sir Thomas Beecham encountered one of them on the British Railway. The noted conductor had deliberately chosen a non-smoking car. In came a lady who opened her handbag and took out a package of cigarettes. She turned to Sir Thomas saying, "You won't mind if I smoke." He answered, "No, Madam, and you won't mind if I become sick." She became haughty: "Sir, I don't think you know who I am. I am one of the Ministers' wives." With that precision in timing of which all great conducting consists, Sir Thomas replied: "Madam, even if you were the Minister's only wife, I should still be sick."

Mr. Chairman, you did tell me that usually your speakers said a less whimsical word or two before sitting down, and I should like to do so. It is perhaps even more important that something serious be said at Thanksgiving this year than it was on some happier Thanksgivings in the past. I have in mind the many disconcerting things that we have heard and read about ourselves in recent weeks and days. In this particular season of American history, all of us can readily think of things that we are not thankful for.

Recent allegations have been made which are disturbing in their nature and ominous in their implications.* While we do not yet know the full truth of these worrisome reports, they are, as the White House said yesterday, "abhorrent to the conscience of all Americans." Observing the caution required when facts are not yet proved, and when trials have not yet been held, we nevertheless can say:

For what the Vietnam War is causing some Americans to do to other human beings in the theater of hostilities, we are not thankful.

For what this war has caused some Americans to do to other Americans at home, we are not thankful either.

For the emotions that the war has unleashed, for the divisiveness it has engendered, for the passions it has aroused, we are emphatically not thankful.

Even as we try to distinguish between the undisciplined horrors that occur in war and contrast them with a deliberate policy of terror, we cannot be grateful for the loathsome necessity to make the distinction.

Nor, as we struggle for balance and proportion, are we thankful for the distasteful predicament we face, of trying to put outrages into perspective without condoning the outrages themselves.

As always in dark moments of our national life, solace can be found by returning to the best in the American tradition. Some may have been helped in the American Church this morning as we joined in singing the unfamiliar second stanza of one of our most familiar hymns:

---

* Accounts of the My Lai massacre in Vietnam had dominated the weekly news, and the British ambassador in Washington had been called home for consultation.

"Oh beautiful for heroes proved,

In liberating strife,

Who more than self their country loved,

And mercy more than life!

"America! America!

God mend thy every flaw.

Confirm thy soul in self-control,

Thy liberty in law!"

Nor should we forget that during a week dominated by headlines about alleged atrocities, President Nixon, in the constructive exercise of the power and initiative of the Presidency, has taken several potentially significant steps: his announcement on Tuesday of the complete renunciation of biological weapons and his reaffirmed renunciation of the first use of chemical weapons; his request for Senate approval of the Geneva protocol whose objectives we have long favored; the ratification last Monday by the United States and the Soviet Union of the Nuclear Non-Proliferation Treaty; and the opening in Helsinki of the strategic arms limitation talks between the US and the USSR.

Nor in a larger context, should we Americans ever forget that we still share certain advantages from history as we enter the final third of the twentieth century. Some of them are worthy of restatement:

First, as our British forefathers were the earliest to understand, we constitute the first major power to arise in the West with an explicitly anti-colonial tradition. Nothing can take this credential from us, except our own waywardness in departing from that heritage.

Second, we are the first major power whose own ethnic base is genuinely diverse, representing cultural strains from around the world. We have borrowed sufficiently heavily from others so that they, looking at us, almost inevitably find something of themselves coming back. In the most un-patronizing sense, everybody else has a stake in us.

Third, we stand in the front line of experimentation in pushing forward the horizons of modernization and development—from north to south and from earth to space—as though we were led by Adam Smith's Invisible Hand to be agents provocateurs of environmental change and technological progress.

Fourth, our very pragmatism and adaptability leave us ideologically unencumbered by the so-called 'revolutionary' orthodoxies of a century ago, which like Marxism-Leninism, are now so embarrassing to those with a vested interest in outworn creeds as well as to those who continue to pay lip service to litanies that no longer turn people on.

Fifth, just as countless Americans project themselves outward into the new century, so much of the world simultaneously aspires to become more like America. Pluralism proliferates, distinctiveness declines, and the potential rises for all the reciprocities of working relationships.

Sixth, our very transparency can be an asset. Americans are not good at fooling themselves or others. When we try, we fail. This characteristic leads to long term accountability--to less fraud and more frankness; to less contrivance and more openness.

Seventh, despite all its temporary inconveniences for policy makers, the tentativeness bred by pluralism can also be an asset. It can be a means of reassurance that in America tomorrow is always another day, a useful reason for others to decide against smugness, haste, apprehension, or final write-offs. It can promote world politics on a mass dimension. It leads us Americans to do more of what comes naturally--to interest ourselves in our fellow citizens of the world, confident that while governments come and go, the people go on forever.

Eighth. All of these elements conspire to promote certain other positive imperatives; impulses toward the intelligibility required for a broad public understanding of issues; impulses toward consultation and dialogue, official and unofficial, on multi-channel frequencies; impulses to universalize values, to move up and out of culture-bound parochialisms; impulses to draw upon others' successes as well as our own; impulses toward change –to welcome it, to champion it; and finally impulses toward acceptance of the old proposition that peace is indivisible, and consequently toward a willingness to take this proposition seriously enough to fight to establish livable terms for peaceful coexistence at the cost of considerable harassment, blood, treasure, and even guilt.

Over the generations American have grown accustomed to pointed questions asked by our friends in England. Thus Thomas Huxley challenged us a century ago:

"I cannot say that I am in the slightest degree impressed by your bigness, or your material resources, as such. Size is not grandeur and territory does not make a nation. The great issue about which hangs the terror of overhanging fate, is what are you going to do with all these things?"

What are we going to do with them? Today this is a question which Americans are asking of one another more insistently than ever before. We can, if we choose, do as Huxley's Queen Victoria herself used to do. She had the faculty of letting things pass—Acts of Parliament and other things. Letting things pass is a highly valuable attribute at the right time and place.

Or we can, if we wish, go out into this generation to stand for the truths that man's future on earth need not be cancelled; that we need not resign ourselves to catastrophe; that our political ingenuity may still rescue us from ruin; that our ethical standards still are here; that building the institutions of peace is worth the effort; and that we can have a world made safe for those things most centrally and lastingly human.

Over the long haul, I have little doubt which course we shall choose. In that sense, and in that faith on Thanksgiving Day, I think we too can say, as Lincoln was able to say when our Civil War was at its height: "Thanks to all-- to the Great Republic, for the principles it lives by and keeps alive, for Man's vast future--thanks to all."

Balliol Broad Street

Sheldonian on Broad Street

Balliol Library

Balliol Dining Hall

Balliol First Year Room

Balliol Second Year Room

Balliol Barge

TLH Returns to Balliol

Tea on the River

Balliol Crew

Eights Week on the River

Punting

LEAVES FROM THE JOURNAL
OF OUR LIFE IN IMAGINE
Toastmaster's Remarks at the Annual
Oxford-Cambridge Dinner
Shoreham Hotel, Washington, D.C.
April 11, 1972

THE GRACE: Ladies and Gentlemen, pray silence and rise for The Grace which will be said by the chairman of your dinner committee, the Honorable Robert Hale of Trinity College, Oxford. Congressman Hale.

THE LOYAL TOASTS: I call upon the British Minister in Washington, Donald Claude Tebbit, C.M.G., of Trinity Hall, Cambridge, to propose the Toast to the President. Mr. Tebbit.

I call upon the Chairman of the Senate Foreign Relations Committee, the Honorable J. William Fulbright of Pembroke, Oxford, to propose the Toast to the Queen. Senator Fulbright.

Ladies and Gentlemen, before you smoke, kindly consider four noteworthy developments since our dinner last year: (1) the Royal College of physicians has belatedly discovered the dangers of smoking; (2) the British Health Education Council is now financing a nationwide advertisement urging you to give up smoking if you wish to retain your sex appeal; (3) a Council spokesman has recently announced that "these adverts are having a great effect on the British public;" and (4) a group called Action on Smoking and Health (or ASH) has declared Princess Anne herself to be the winner of the "Non-Smoker of the Year" award. If you remain unimpressed by these developments, you may now light up.

I begin with a goodwill appetizer which in effect gives you twice a much for your money. This unearned increment consists of a brief report on the Oxford-Cambridge dinner held in New York on March 23rd. I think no one would argue that it would be worthwhile going to New York just to attend their dinner. But finding myself already there at my Carnegie office, I went. (My state of mind reminded me of the notice in the college porter's lodge: "Meeting tonight on Schizophrenia" with the graffiti underneath "I've half a mind to attend.")

Some will also recall the despairing Dean of an Oxford College who was driven to distraction by undergraduate confusion, and who therefore began his prayers by saying: "Paradoxical as it must seem to Thee, O Lord." A veteran of our Washington dinners would quickly have been struck by the paradoxes in New York. Here one never speaks of Cambridge and Oxford. One always speaks of Oxford and Cambridge. But paradoxically, right here on the cover of the New York program, you can see that the emblems of the universities are reversed: Cambridge is plainly precedent on the left, Oxford uneasily subsequent on the right.

This protocolary snafu was corrected inside the New York menu, where the university seals appear in their proper places. (I should explain that the discolorations on my souvenir menu are not the bloodstains which they appear to be, but only a tribute to the bad aiming of the red wine pourers at the Harvard Club where the dinner was held.)

The meal itself left a good deal to be desired, and someone from the UK Mission to the UN, seated opposite, alluded to Disraeli's remark upon the arrival of champagne at a fashionable dinner: "Thank God for something warm."

When the time came for the loyal toasts, some of us thought we heard the New York toastmaster say: "I rise to propose a toast to the President of the United States and/ or Her Majesty, the Queen." That seemed to leave everybody feeling satisfactorily ambivalent, especially the Indian ambassador who was the guest of honor. He was there, of course, in violation of Dr. Kissinger's express instructions via the Anderson papers that "the Indian Ambassador is not to be treated at too high a level."

That "certain coolness" to Indians, recently prescribed at the National Security Council meeting, was nowhere in evidence at the New York dinner. People there behaved as though they were beyond the reach of the NSC system. Indeed Ambassador Jha was received warmly, as one who had come in from the cold.

Perhaps carried away by the warmth of the ambassador's welcome, the toastmaster then allowed himself to say that Mr. Jha "went down from Balliol in 1930." Cheers and merriment thereupon broke out, since the program plainly listed him as a Trinity, Cambridge, man. Subsequently we were told that he had studied under Maynard Keynes himself, who was described as an earlier equivalent of Arthur Burns.

The 118th boat race had not yet been run, but another victory for Cambridge was everywhere anticipated. Reference was made to dark blues going to chapel singing "Lead Kindly Light." (Perhaps some pervasive Manhattan influence has been at work even here in the selection of tonight's exclusively light blue table candles.) We also learned that last winter the New York Rhodes Scholar selection committee lost a good man whose priorities took him to Cairo, instead of Oxford, to row on the Nile in a tournament sponsored by the Egyptian police.

ITT metaphors inevitably crept into the boat race speculation. Use was made of Senator Goldwater's press release that afternoon defending Mr. Kleindienst as being "beyond approach." This was regarded as an apt description of the probable position of the Cambridge boat the following Saturday.

So much for the New York dinner. An habitué of these Washington celebrations, where six years ago we put away the boat race along with other childish things, would naturally begin to think complacent thoughts about cultural lag and effortless superiority.

Here we regularly go in for more serious fare. This year when I was told that I was to be your toastmaster yet again, it was obliquely mentioned that a recent returnee from an official assignment in London might naturally be expected to make his own contribution to the growing body of revelations in Anglo-American relations— especially since, up to now, the disclosures have largely come from the British side.

Thus, their thirty-year rule has already permitted us to learn what Sir Ronald Lindsay, British ambassador here in the 1930s, was really telling his superiors in Whitehall. Today when we review Sir Ronald's pithy sketches, we must take care to keep them firmly embedded in the historical context in which they were written. You can see why.

On the President: "A baffling character...a poor judge of men. He appears to be extremely obstinate and to dislike opposition. His intellectual powers are really only moderate and his knowledge of certain subjects, particularly finance and economics, is superficial."

On the former President: "Probably the most abused man in the United States, without the power to turn on a cheerful smile, or to make the humorous remark which means so much to a publicity-ridden country."

On the Chairman of the Foreign Relations Committee: "He is almost an ideal Senator, with no desire to put forward constructive ideas, but always anxious to so frame his utterances that he will afterwards be able to prove that he was right and everyone else was wrong."

On the Chairman of the Democratic National Committee: "Some regard him as 'honest,' others as a politician of Machiavellian subtlety. The correct estimate of him is probably midway between these two extremes."

For good measure the British ambassador added his thoughts on two, then prominent, American publishers. William Randolph Hearst was an Anglophobe, the ambassador wrote, because "in England he counts for nothing and is systematically, and rightly ignored." The Chicago Tribune's Colonel Robert McCormick was "stubborn, slow-thinking, and bellicose, with a definite anti-British bias, still resentful of the canings he received whilst a schoolboy at Eton."

"Better shred than dead" may be the motto at ITT, but let us be thankful that there was no Foreign Office shredding machine in service in London thirty-three years ago.

Emboldened by such precedents, let me now contribute my own widow's mite to the growing literature in the field. It consists of a preliminary account of my own Anglo-American assignment, undertaken on behalf of President Nixon in our embassy in London in the years of our Lord 1969 and 1970; of the independence of the United States the 194th and 195th; and of the ambassadorship of Walter H. Annenberg the last half of the first and the first half of the second.

For the format of the remarks that follow I am indebted to one of the forgotten works of the nineteenth century, a book by Queen Victoria herself, entitled "Leaves from the Journal of Our Life in the Highlands." Her book was once on everyone's parlor table. "We authors…" Disraeli remarked at Windsor. For reasons that will presently appear, the title for tonight's purposes should be amended to read: "Leaves from the Journal of Our Life In Imagine." But otherwise the credit is the Queen's.

My subject matter, like hers, lends itself to the style of artless prattle which the royal author employs in her journal. There, for example, one has frequent glimpses of Her Majesty on the deck of the Victoria and Albert, dividing her time between suffering storms at sea and straining to discern the misty outlines of what she calls the "Scotch coast." Such were the scenes that led, no doubt, to the story that one day when the royal yacht was struck by an exceptionally huge wave, the Queen sent for the Captain and said: "That must not occur again."

Once on land, there were Gaelic games at Braemar by day and games of whist at Balmoral by night. There were visits to Fingal's Cave and much reading aloud of "The Lay of the Last Minstrel." Albert, dressed in the Stuart plaid, shot stags, while the Queen rode her pony which was "beautifully, carefully led by that most attentive of servants, Brown."

The Prince Consort was constantly driven to allusion. Thus, he found that the people of what he called "Edinburg" also looked like Germans. Glen Ogle resembled an Alpine pass. The quays of Glasgow evoked memories of Paris. Perth reminded him of Basel. The plethora of such associations proves that at least a hundred years ago the British royal family was ready for Europe.

The Queen's journal also had a nice common touch. Typically she wrote: "We were always in the habit of conversing with the Highlanders, with whom one comes so much in contact in the Highlands." At the end there were always the clumps of sad-eyed village loyalists at Balmoral station singing "Will ye nae come back again," as the royal train pulled out for London and Her Britannic Majesty sat back in her railway carriage, thumbing through the Almanach de Gotha, contemplating brides and grooms for her many children and grandchildren.

If anything, the raw material for my journal is even more exotic than hers. But her preface can hardly be improved upon and I accept it as my own:

"This little work does not make any pretension to be more than such a record of the impressions received by the Royal Author as might hereafter recall to her own mind the scenes and circumstances of so much pleasure. All references to political questions, or to the affairs of government, have, for obvious reasons, been studiously omitted. The (work) is mainly confined to the natural expressions of a mind throwing itself, with a delight rendered keener by the rarity of its opportunities, into the enjoyment of a life removed, for the moment, from the pressure of public cares… (Hence) in every page the writer describes what she thinks and feels, rather than what she might be expected to think and feel."

What is more, I can even adopt without change the words of the Queen's dedication which reads: "To the dear memory of him who made the life of the writer bright and happy, these simple records are lovingly and gratefully inscribed." Queen Victoria, of course, was thinking of Albert. I am thinking of Annenberg.

(Leaves from the Journal of our Life in Imagine.)

In England, the year 1969 began in a manner no more or less eventful than other years. Careful readers of The Times around the second week in February, however, came upon a letter called "Accents in the Close" from Mr. Robin Bryer. "Sir, today I heard the first American in the Cathedral Close here in Winchester. I think this is a record, probably indicative of the effect of a mild winter on migration patterns. Yours faithfully, Robin Bryer, the Wykeham Arms, Winchester, February 10."

That was followed a few days later by a response under the same heading from Canon A. S. Gribble. "Sir, spring must be late in Winchester. The first Americans appeared in the Precincts here on January 28. Yours faithfully, Arthur Gribble, Prebendal House, Minster Precincts, Peterborough."

But in America, the spring of 1969 was rather different. We all had a new Republican President, and each of us reacted to that phenomenon in our own special way. The new President himself reacted by setting about quickly to do what he could for Anglo-American relations.

Nixon-watchers had long been aware of his pro-British proclivities, including his admiration for Lord Palmerston in the nineteenth century and Sir Winston Churchill in the twentieth. It is true that Palmerston once said that dining was the soul of diplomacy. It is also true that Churchill once said that the British empire was built on the proposition: never trust the man on the spot. Some observers, putting these two maxims together, leaped to the logic of Mr. Nixon's choice of ambassador to the Court of St. James. In any case, when it was announced in late February, the response was electric. "Ambassadors don't often come as colourful as this," said the Daily Mail headline greeting his appointment.

Meanwhile, I myself was preparing to accommodate our national change in regime. I had prepared to return to unofficial life. Brookings awaited. Then the totally unexpected happened. One day after briefing Secretary Rogers I thought I heard him say:

"Who would want to go to Brookings? Why don't you go to London as Minister in the Embassy? We have a new man there, you know, and you have had a lot of experience with the British. They also have a Labour Government, and you once worked for the Senate Labor Committee." I replied rather weakly, that I had never made that connection myself. However one thing led to another. Ultimately it was offer, acceptance, contract.

I have been told that a few days later a Balliol don was partaking in some table talk in the Assistant Secretaries' dining room. Somebody there was pursuing the elusive idea that the professor had taught me in a tutorial twenty years ago. There was obviously no immediate flicker of recognition. After being reminded twice of my name and the eminence of my new position, the Oxford visitor suddenly said: "Oh yes, him. I say, he's done disappointingly well."

As my wife, Jean, and I began preparing for a summer move, I began reading the British press with greater care than usual. As a precaution, I also took out a subscription to the Philadelphia Inquirer. Jean enrolled in the professional training course at the Foreign Service Institute, which providentially included a seminar entitled "How to Handle Difficult Situations."

It was from that seminar that she brought home, one night, a singular document entitled "The Role of the Deputy Chief of Mission's Wife," a pamphlet prepared by the Association of American Foreign Service Women. Selected highlights must be shared, for as Oscar Wilde said about the death of Dickens' Little Nell, you would have to have a heart of stone to experience it without laughing. It began:

"A wife learns from her husband that he has just been assigned Deputy Chief of Mission to 'Post Imagine.' The role of DCM is new to them both. Since time is short, she proceeds immediately to find out all she can about 'Imagine.' If she and her husband are in Washington, her husband can get answers to many of her questions from the country desk officer. Book lists from the public library also provide plenty of essential reading.

"If her husband is advised that it is appropriate, she calls on 'opposite number' wives at the embassy of 'Imagine' in Washington, alert to ask questions and get helpful suggestions. For example, if she has the space, she may wish to take along some books in simple English as well as materials for teaching English to adults.

"Later when the DCM travels around 'Imagine,' an indication from his wife that she is interested in seeing something special-- whether a hospital, a school, or some botanical phenomenon-- is always appreciated…If some of the food may be strange or different, a willingness to take a taste and a warm smile are in order…Of course the DCM's wife has to be like Caesar's wife in all respects--above and beyond suspicion. Yet all of this must be done without infringing in any way on the role of the Ambassador's wife…

"And now, polished, packed, and prepared, with calling cards taking up precious weight, our DCM and his family, briefed and ready, take off for 'Post Imagine.' On arriving, the DCM and his family are likely to be met by photographers and newsmen as well as Embassy representatives…Just as soon as possible, and that means immediately, the DCM's wife calls on her Ambassador's wife…For, from her zest for leadership and 'followership' will spring a richer experience for all."

Before long, as we pondered the implications of followership, the first press reports arrived of the Ambassador's maiden speech at the Pilgrims dinner in London. As a theme, he had chosen to condemn unrest and turmoil in American universities, saying that "the time has come to call an end to giving in to students." "Somewhat curious, considering the occasion," said an unidentified Pilgrim to the New York Times.

A few days later the out-sized figure of Professor Galbraith mounted the MIT commencement platform to hurl a more studied rejoinder:

"I suppose as a former ambassador, I react professionally to Ambasador Annenberg. As our new plenipotentiary in London, he used the occasion of his maiden speech to denounce students--American, not those at the London School of Economics. And speaking out bravely, he demanded an end to permissiveness at Harvard, Swarthmore, and, of course, Berkeley.

"One wondered why. Was it because the British were especially aroused about this issue? That is hard to believe. They are known to suffer our misfortunes with fortitude. Was it that Mr. Annenberg, who has spent a lifetime cultivating the clientele of the Morning Telegraph and the Daily Racing Form, those Gutenberg Bibles of the gambling episcopate, had suddenly at sixty developed a passion for people who could read?" Unquote from Professor Galbraith. (At this point those who take pleasure in the turf would probably want me to note, with regret, today's announcement of the demise of the Morning Telegraph itself.)

By midsummer, hurtling into our midst came news of the BBC's new film on the daily life of Queen Elizabeth II. It was called simply "Royal Family" and was destined to be shown repeatedly to audiences of millions in the UK and around the world. It was clear from the first reports that our Ambassador's performance had securely passed into English social history with a now familiar episode immortalized in technicolor. After alighting from a gilded coach, he hesitantly enters Buckingham Palace, nearly forgets to take off his top hat, and is instructed by Sir Denis Greenhill and palace officials on how to present his credentials. "We all take a pace forward--with our LEFT foot," says one, and then "another little bow when we shake hands."

Later when vis-à-vis, the Queen pleasantly inquires about housing arrangements—or whether the ambassador is perhaps still at Claridge's. He then speaks his now famous lines: "We are in the ambassadorial residence, subject of course to some of the discomfiture as a result of the need for elements of refurbishing and rehabilitation."

At the London preview of the BBC film the enthusiasm following this scene was reportedly "uncontrollable." And the next morning featured an uproar of mirth from Fleet Street and Broadcast House: "Lost in his polysyllables." "Early Chapin." "Genuine American folk-baroque." "The greatest sentence since Beowulf."

Stopping through Washington soon afterwards, the Economic Minister from the embassy raised his eyebrows and asked: "Are you sure you want to come?" With diplomatic dignity, I replied that President Nixon was counting on me and that I couldn't let him down.

As the summer wore on, it was inevitable that the British press would discover that help for the ambassador was on the way. Just how helpful the press itself was going to be may be gleaned from the following account in the Times:

"ANNENBERG'S COMING DEPUTY: It is to the credit of the Nixon administration that it is sending Tom Hughes to London as No. 2 at the American Embassy. As an old Rhodes Scholar at Balliol, Hughes knows and likes England. Moreover his thorough grounding in American policy, and perhaps even his scholarly manner, are clearly intended to strengthen the Embassy which has recently gained a novice."

The Guardian also helped smooth the way:

"POWER AT US ENVOY'S SIDE: If London was surprised at President Nixon's choice of ambassador, it should be delighted with the choice of the man who will share the work at the Embassy—the minister, Mr. Tom Hughes. Unlike his ambassador, Mr. Hughes has wide knowledge of foreign affairs and government as an assistant secretary in the State Department. He employs the English language with a felicity granted to distressingly few Americans."

The Evening Standard then followed suit by striking some helpfully partisan notes:

"NEW MAN: The appointment of the new No. 2 at the American embassy is causing some speculation in diplomatic circles. It is felt that the reason for the appointment may be that the new American Ambassador needs a politically experienced man at his right-hand side…Mr. Hughes is a distinctly different man from the ambassador. He is believed to be a Democrat."

What happened next remains to be told at another time and place. We went, we saw, we entered into diplomatic highlife with the Annenbergs, and we came home at a convenient time, when the British government itself changed hands with Labour giving way to the Tories. Still, I am bound to say that subsequent installments from our Journal belong in a more roisterous milieu like Racing Form itself, rather than the more austere atmosphere of an Oxford-Cambridge dinner.

Just before we left, the Foreign Service inspectors were busily inspecting "Post Imagine." The last item on their Organization and Management Check List posed this question: "Would the establishment of a Consular Agency in lieu of the continuation of the post be a factor in determining whether to close it down?" The accompanying boxes said "yes," "no," or "discuss." I checked "discuss."

In the immediate aftermath of our departure, people asked how it felt to be separated from our good friend, the ambassador. I think they expected a reply like that of Talulah Bankhead's impresario who was once asked a similar question. He had replied that a day away from Talulah was like a month in the country. But at this distance, after leafing once more through the Journal of our Life in Imagine, I think instead of the new film "Is there Sex after Death?" There, after an ambulatory graveyard chat, the answer comes: "No, only affection."

(Introduction of James C. Thomson for the Toast to the Universities.)

It suddenly seems remote, that recent "Week that Was," when the President was implausibly in China and when your next speaker was telling us so much about behavior inside the Forbidden City or behind the Gates of Heavenly Peace,

Those of us who decided that we would get more out of the China trip by remaining at home rather than joining the Presidential entourage, turned out to have one advantage over those who went. There on ABC, no matter whether we turned off our TV at midnight or turned it on at seven a.m., was James C. Thomson, helping Howard K. Smith identify bespectacled Red Army women translators as they flashed onto the screen. While other networks were casting about for more non-events to render their commentators speechless, ABC's viewers received as much deep background as they probably wanted on ex-President Ulysses S. Grant's trip to Peking and other pertinent contextual information.

During his fast-paced career, ABC's China commentator had already proved the truth of former Secretary McNamara's dictum: "Brains on the whole are like hearts—they go where they are appreciated." In 1948-49 when the Chinese Communists seemed unappreciative of Jim's student career at the University of Nanking, he forsook Nanking for New Haven and edited the Yale Daily News instead.

Subsequently, deciding that one of the English universities needed him next, he set about considering which one. Upon discovering that Cecil Rhodes had once advised against writing as a career, using strong words—"Shouldn't do that—it's not a man's work—mere loafing"—Thomson spurned Oxford and went to Cambridge instead.

He was there at Cambridge in 1955 when one of my own far-sighted former employers asked me how to locate another worldly-wise assistant like myself. Providentially we remembered the way such things used to be done. The Cambridge Appointments Board would receive a cable from Calcutta saying: "Send the tramway manager. Classics man preferred." So we sent a cable to Cambridge and in response, in due course, James Thomson arrived.

Some of his skills as a writer come through when you examine his account of himself in "Who's Who" for the years 1956-63: "Asst. to Gov. of Conn., 1956; spl. Asst. to U.S. Congressman, 1959-61; spl. Asst. to Under Sec. State, 1961; spl. Asst. to President's Special Rep. and Adviser on African, Asian and Latin American affairs, 1961-3." So clever is this account that the casual reader might miss the point that Jim was working for the same employer right along, and that it was the latter, not the former, who was having such trouble keeping a job.

Before leaving Washington, however, Jim did achieve an unmatched reputation as an itinerant assistant to one high official after another. In those years when one tried to telephone his current boss--whether the Assistant Secretary for Far Eastern Affairs, or the President's NSC Advisor, or the Vice President himself--it was not uncommon for the receptionist to say: "I'm sorry, but Mr. so-in-so is away from his desk at the moment. However if you will hold the line, I may be able to put you through to Mr. Thomson himself." Every time this happened, I was impressed because, in a manner of speaking, Mr. Thomson had once worked for me as well.

Today as Senior Lecturer at Harvard's East Asian Research Center, he must be making his own plans to re-enter China as soon as the invitation comes. Meanwhile, we can only guess with what envy he reads of our next official mission to Peking. It begins next week, and consists of our dinner companion, the Senate Minority Leader, Mr. Scott, (who reportedly will be looking for a set of Chinese porcelains embellished with a Balliol coat of arms) and his colleague and supporter, the Majority Leader who is also an old China hand and who incidentally tomorrow becomes the father-in-law of a Cambridge don.

They even intend to report to the Foreign Relations Committee, which must gratify yet another Senator here tonight. This is all a considerable advance from the 1940s when Senator Wherry of Nebraska was saying: "With God's help, we will lift Shanghai up and up, ever up, until it is just like Kansas City."

In the winter of 1968-9 when he was waiting to take office, Mr. Nixon told us: "For the first time in twenty years we're going to have a piano player in the White House. I play the piano, for example, Christmas carols…I can play all of the old timers, but I've got to learn the new tunes, the swingers."

Now Mr. Nixon's enthusiasm for the piano is just one more interest which binds him to Chairman Mao. Mao has addressed the subject in his essay called "Learn to play the piano." On pages 110-11 of his little red book he tells us: "In playing the piano, all ten fingers are in motion. It won't do to move some fingers only and not others. But if all ten fingers press down at once, there is no melody. To produce good music, the ten fingers should move in coordination. Wherever there is a problem, we must put our finger on it. This is a method we must master. Some play the piano well and some badly, and there is a great difference in the melodies they produce. We must learn to play the piano well."

I now call upon a man who plays the piano well—at times, indeed, with all ten fingers, just as Mao recommends. He is James C. Thomson, Jr., of Clare College, Cambridge, who will propose the toast to the Universities.

(Introduction of Alastair Buchan for the Response from the Universities.)

Your final speaker has a notable habit of presiding over institutions which suddenly change their names. Thus, he was the first director of the Institute for Strategic Studies. It now styles itself the International Institute for Strategic Studies. Only three years ago he was appointed the commandant of the Imperial Defence College. Today it calls itself the Royal College of Defence Studies. Now as the Montague Burton Professor of International Relations, he is once more associated with what has hitherto been known as Oxford University, and, even more alarmingly, with Balliol College itself. One hopes they are on guard against the name changes that Alastair Buchan's arrival normally portends.

As is known, Mr. Buchan is the son of John Buchan, the celebrated author, Governor General of Canada, and first Baron Tweedsmuir. As such, Alastair was the son of a famous father and hence he might have qualified for Magdalen. I allude to the conversation there in the 1920s between Sir Herbert Warren, then the college President, and the new undergraduate, Prince Chichbu, son of the emperor of Japan.

During the matriculation audience, granted to all new Magdalen men, there was more than the usual amount of genteel fencing marked by awkward pauses. Finally the President bluntly inquired: "Where did you get an odd name like Chichibu? What would that be in English?" The Japanese prince mentioned deferentially that people had Japanese names in Japan, not all of which were easily translatable. However, if an English equivalent were insisted upon, he supposed that "Chicibu" could roughly be rendered as "son of God." There was another pause while the President of Magdalen reflected. "Young man," he said thoughtfully, "I have no doubt that in due course you will find the sons of many other prominent men in residence in the college."

Perhaps, for this very reason, the undergraduate Alastair Buchan settled on Christ Church instead. But what a further tribute to the maturing wisdom of the intervening years that now, back in Oxford, he is at long last at Balliol where he should have been all along. As far as one hears, the dominant group at the House still consists of beaglers, sports-car drivers, champagne-party givers, and future Tory MPs. I am told that there was a brief period after World War I when behavior even at Balliol resembled Christ Church. Indeed there was a Balliol club named the Histeran Prateran, whose members put themselves to real discomfort by living a day in reverse: getting up in evening dress, drinking whiskey, smoking cigars and playing cards, then at ten a.m. dining backward, starting with savouries and ending with soup.

But that was a brief post-armistice interlude. Balliol quickly regained its sobriety, and for decades now Balliol men have been able to resume concentrating on those things that matter most: surveying their own achievements and generally cultivating an awareness of Balliol outside the college walls.

In between Christ Church and his recent translation to Balliol, Alastair Buchan pursued a varied career. He is a dutiful husband who has nevertheless postponed celebrating his thirtieth wedding anniversary to be with us tonight. He was a distinguished soldier with the Canadian Army in World War II; a journalist for several years on both sides of the Atlantic with the Economist and the Observer; and director for eleven years of I.I.S.S. He once did a biography of Bagehot, and has lately written or edited books with titles like "War in Modern Society," "China and the Peace of Asia," and "Europe's Futures, Europe's Choices." Ten years ago he wrote a book on NATO, which he revises as necessary.

All this led to a burst of consultation with Henry Kissinger in the winter of 1968-9 as the latter prepared to take over the White House. Indeed I remember, in the spring of 1969, overhearing a cocktail party conversation which went something like this: "Well, now that Nixon's first 100 days are over, tell me two good things that he has done." Answer: "He has brought Alastair Buchan into the White House and kept the Marines out of Belfast." Perhaps it is going to far to credit Mr. Buchan with the authorship of the Nixon Doctrine, but there are those who think he has a better claim to it than all but one or two others. Despite his rumored authorship, he was not above asking visiting Americans to come and explain the Doctrine at the Imperial Defence College—perhaps rather excessive of him in the circumstances.

His Who's Who account refers with studied casualness to "articles in Foreign Affairs, etc." No wonder the Council on Foreign Relations periodically summons him to New York, as they are currently doing, to deliver three of their endowed lectures. I don't know which one of them he will give us tonight, but having heard the first two, it gives me great pleasure to ask the Honorable Alastair Buchan of Christ Church and Balliol to reply to the Toast to the Universities.

ADJOURNMENT: It no longer goes without saying that God, love, and Anglo-American relations are the three most important things in life. Yet more than enough has been said here tonight to demonstrate that if all three of these things must tarnish, the hope still exists that they will tarnish in the proper order. Thank you and good night.

THE EFFICIENT SECRET OF OXFORD
The Response to the Toast
American Rhodes Scholars 75th Anniversary
Dinner at the University Club, New York, NY
September 25, 1978

When I was approached about speaking here tonight, I demurred. Perhaps George Bernard Shaw's exchange with Lady Sutherland would again be pertinent. She sent him an invitation which read: "Lady Sutherland. At home Monday, September 25th." He sent back a card: "Mr. Shaw. Likewise."

Playing for time, I asked who else might be coming. There was a deferential mention of Professor Merriam, who matriculated in 1904. I agreed that his presence seemed eminently fitting for a 75th anniversary, but would there possibly be any of the younger generation attending?

As a matter of fact, came the reply, the others at the high table would be: the Master of Balliol; Mr. Barber of Kansas and Balliol; Mr. Bodine of Connecticut and Balliol; and Mr. Mendenhall of Wisconsin and Balliol. So it was hoped that the response would come from Balliol as well.

Indeed, the event was shaping up as a kind of impromptu Balliol Gaudy. Boola Boola Balliol. Well rowed Balliol. A Balliol festival to follow in the wake of Venice,

Salzburg, and Edinburgh. I said I had long adjusted to the inexorable process of Balliolization. Others have noted that Balliol men are marked not only by their achievements but by their awareness of Balliol. Predominance at a 75th Rhodes anniversary celebration seemed incontestably appropriate, so I concluded that it would be churlish of me to refuse.

It is true that I have just returned from England. I am therefore in a position to pass on a few tidbits which may not have reached readers of the strike-bound New York papers:

The Foreign Office has announced that it has no plans to ask the French government for the return to England of the entrails of Henry V, as demanded by a Labour MP.

Lady Longforn has written to the Sunday Times to say: "I try never to go out for lunch any more. It takes such a lot of time--four hours the other day."

Rear Admiral Morgan-Giles, MP for Winchester, has announced that although the pay of the Navy is not up to the task it performs, sailors do not want to be represented by a trade union. "Generally speaking," the admiral said, "they would rather starve."

Lord George-Brown, the former Foreign Minister, is standing for the European Parliament because, he explains, "Britain is a country which has no twentieth century indigenous resources."

Hugh MacDiarmid, the Scottish nationalist poet, has just died. His obituaries noted that in his Who's Who account under "Recreation" he listed simply "Anglophobia."

The Duke of Atholl has told the House of Lords: "We have become rather ashamed of the grouse moor image, unnecessarily."

At the Sandhurst graduation exercises, a foreign correspondent for the Daily Telegraph praised foreign governments for sending their young men to Sandhurst instead of to Oxford. "A Sandhurst education," he said, "is more reliable than an Oxford one when the coup comes."

The Queen Mother has just become Warden of the Cinque Ports, a post which in the past has sometimes fallen to ex-prime ministers. She now has responsibility for all whales washed up on the southeast coast.

The Arab takeover of London is being commemorated nightly at the Apollo Theatre in a play entitled: "Shut your eyes and think of England." The extent of the takeover will become apparent when the palace releases the next Ramadan Honours list.

Above all, Britain is pleased with the publication of its latest contribution to the Special Relationship. This is the new book by the editor of Punch, Alan Coren of Wadham and Yale. He calls it "The Peanut Papers."

It consists of a collection of letters of advice and commentary written from Plains, Georgia, by Miz Lillian Carter to Jimmy, Billy, Rosalyn, Amy, and other members of her family including Great-Uncle Stinkweed Carter, Aunt Eulalia Moonshine Carter, Great-Grandpaw Faggot Carter, Cuzin Nehemiah Honest Carter, Uncle Snob Carter III, Private Chickenhaid Carter, Cuzin Practically Reverend Stonewall Carter (Founduh and Patriarch of Thuh Fust Church of Christ the Crapshootuh), and Cuzin Elizabeth Two Carter, otherwise Queen of England, whose recent genealogical link to Miz Lillian has just been unearthed.

Miz Lillian's letter to the Queen begins: "Deah Cuzin Elizabeth Two Carter: another few yeahs an, who knows, y'all could be thuh Queen of somewhere real big, such as Chinuh or Los Angeles, it's all jest a question of keepin right in theah an pitchin."

The Peanut Papers also contain practical suggestions for a direct Concorde linkup from London to Plains; as well as for handling Peter Jay, Andy Young, and the "Raid-Black-Female-Gay-Zionist-Longhaired-Forn-Menace" generally.

But of course even in London, the sensational appointment of the new master of Balliol was still the chief subject of notoriety. I found myself discussing it at a lunch in the City. "There has always been a subversive kind of succession at Balliol," one old boy said. "First there was Wyclif and his Lollards in the 14th century. Then there was Jowett and all his freethinking, and then Lindsay and his Labour friends, right up to Christopher Hill, an admitted Marxist who claims to have changed."

"Put yourself in Hill's shoes," said another. How would you feel, as an unfrocked Communist Master of Balliol, to be told that you would be succeeded by an unfrocked priest?" "I suppose," said a third, "much the same way that Doctor Johnson felt about his dictionary." Remind me, I said. The exchange:

Boswell: "What would you say, Sir, if you were told that your Dictionary would be superseded by one written by a Scotch Nonconformist, living at Oxford?"

Johnson: "Sir, in order to be facetious, it is not necessary to be indecent."

Now Jowett once told the college assembled in Hall: "I should like every man to feel hereafter that the years he spent here constituted the happiest as well as the most profitable period of his life, though I should not expect him to say it in the presence of his wife."

I feel bound to ask the forbearance of the wives who are present for the ambivalent feelings which this evening must arouse in them. However, it isn't the first time such forbearance has been sought. In 1861 when an earlier Thomas Hughes was writing his less than immortal book, "Tom Brown at Oxford," he too felt obliged to protect himself:

"Dear readers of the gentler sex! You, I know, will pardon the enthusiasm which stirs our pulses, now in sober middle age, as we call up again the memories of this, the most exciting sport of our boyhood." He then launched into his chapter on the pleasures of the river with famous lines like: "All rowed fast, but none so fast as stroke."

Women have plagued our scholarship story from the beginning. John Ruskin is the man who is generally credited with inspiring Rhodes the undergraduate in the 1870s with his vision of Britain's world mission. Ruskin refused to allow women into his art lectures: "I cannot let the bonnets in…."

But now pulses quicken and not only at the recollection of the boat race. Of the seventy some Rhodes Scholars now at Oxford, twenty four are women. Already there is an American Rhodes Scholar letterwoman playing field hockey for Jesus. And the best is yet to be. In Michaelmas term next year, the gates of most of the remaining male colleges will swing open to women, including Balliol. Only Merton, Rhodes' own Oriel, and Christ Church will still be holding out. It may take another act of Parliament to move Merton and Oriel. As for the House, you never know which way those canons will vote.

Balliol's preparations for the arrival of women cannot be too exacting. Presumably Mr. Mendenhall, as the former president of Smith, has been able to brief our new master on some of the probable hurdles. But Balliol has a special revisionist problem entailing the rewriting of famous texts. Familiar phrases take on new meanings. The well-known saying that life is just one Balliol man after another--amply proved again tonight--will now presumably have to go.

Or, consider the probable fate of Hilaire Belloc's legendary lines "To the Balliol Men still in Africa." A master of Balliol as late as 1954 allowed himself to say that this poem "lies at the very heart of the whole Balliol matter." All Balliol men can recite it from memory, but it will be awkward for the new Balliol women to join in:

"Here is a House that armours a man

With the eyes of a boy and the heart of a ranger

And a laughing way in the teeth of the world

And a holy hunger and thirst for danger.

Balliol made me, Balliol fed me.

Whatever I had she gave me again.

And the best of Balliol loved and led me

God be with you, Balliol men."

God be with you, Balliol girls. Floreat DAMUS de Balliolo. Life will be just one Balliol woman after another. Beautiful Balliol! (Nobody ever said that before.) Even the usually taciturn warden of Rhodes House, Sir Edgar Williams, at lunch in the Balliol SCR, speculated gleefully about the prospect of the first wedding between two Balliol Rhodes Scholars. "We ought to put that god-forsaken chapel to some use, don't you think?"

Who knows, with the arrival of the women and the new master, even though he has reverted to a lay state, there may be a revival of religion itself at Balliol. As Jowett told a young lady years ago, "You must believe in God, my dear, despite what the clergymen say."

Apart from what Professor Merriam in his discretion cares to disclose, until recently we could only speculate about how the Cecil Rhodes mystique affected the early Rhodes Scholars. Suddenly a book fell into my hands for twenty-five cents at the annual State Department book sale. It is a biography of Rhodes by Sir Thomas Fuller, KCMG, published by Longmans Green, Bombay and Calcutta, 1910, and dedicated to the Rhodes Scholars at Oxford. One of them from Oklahoma obtained it that very year. The Oklahoman affixed his personal bookplate inside the cover. It was adorned with a huge buffalo head and a coat of arms rather ominously titled, "The Time to Come."

Years later, Dorothy Thompson, a devotee of the podium, used to tell a story about her arrival at Tulsa, Oklahoma. At the station she was asked by the young man who met her what her lecture topic would be. "The Decay of Western Values", she replied. His face fell. "Oh, Miss Thompson," he said, "western values have only just come to Tulsa, Oklahoma."

Our Oklahoma Rhodes Scholar's heavy annotations from 1910, however, show how wrong this intelligence was. Here are a few samples:

The knighted author's text: "I must ask the reader to remember that I write about Mr. Rhodes at a time of life when memory is apt to fail, and also that I have had no opportunity of verifying recollections by public records." Our Rhodes Scholar's marginal note: "Good."

Text: "I do not propose to play to Cecil Rhodes the part of Boswell." Margin: "Who could?"

Text: "Mr. Rhodes used to remark playfully: 'Don't try and birdlime me onto a party stick!' He trusted character when he came to know it." Margin: "What else is there to trust?"

Text: "Rhodes was always Rhodes however he was dressed. His well-loved Oxford tweeds suited him best, but he was quite at home in ordinary evening dress." Margin: "Milton listed all the great qualities. Rhodes had most of these to a high level, and all to some extent."

Text: "'I am not at all well,' Rhodes remarked, 'and I am off for a motor tour in Scotland to pick up strength.'" Margin: "My God! What a way to pick up strength!"

Text: "Mr. Rhodes received a great ovation at his beloved Oxford, when the D.C.L. was conferred on him and his intimate friend, Lord Kitchener. He told me with almost childish glee that the reception he had received exceeded even that of Lord Kitchener." Margin: "Who could help that?"

Text: "It was decided, in spite of his connection with the Jameson Raid, that Rhodes should retain his position amongst the Privy Councilors...a decision arrived at, not only by the ministers of the Crown, but by Her Majesty." Margin: "Too good a man to ditch."

Text: "Rhodes boasted that he had read every life of Napoleon, but he did not talk very much about him, at least to me." Margin: "Smart fellow."

Text: "Every living man," Rhodes said, "should be a worker. No idlers, no mere dreamers, should be tolerated." Margin: "You bet. If any man work not let him not eat."

One thinks instinctively of the opening pages of "The American" by Henry James: "An observer would have had no difficulty in determining the local origin of this undeveloped connoisseur...(He) had that typical vagueness which is not vacuity, that blankness which is not simplicity, that look of being committed to nothing in

67

particular, of standing in an attitude of general hospitality to the chances of life, of being very much at one's own disposal, so characteristic of the American type…."

We cannot celebrate a Rhodes anniversary wholeheartedly, because the Founder does not lend himself comfortably to unstinted praise. To put the best cast upon it, he was a man of great gifts and great flaws—a man of paradoxes who left paradoxical legacies. He had stunted visions and capacious ones—"painting the map red," "philanthropy plus 5%," and universal peace.

Like Bismarck he "wanted to make history, not write it." Darwinian, jingoist, and empire builder, he was a colossus with feet of clay. Although others like him viewed the world as a joint-stock company, who but Rhodes would have thought of basing an empire on the sale of engagement rings?

Like some prominent Americans of his day, he believed in direct action and in living dangerously. He was an American in his impatience and in his ideas of size. He even had American emulators. It was the heyday of flag-raising and saber- rattling for us as well. Manifest Destiny suddenly gave us Cuba, the Philippines, Puerto Rico, and Panama, not exactly in a fit of absent-mindedness.

After his and Jameson's famous raid, Rhodes lost the Cape prime minister-ship, was censured in the House of Commons, and even barred from the Travelers Club. But Mother Oxford came to his rescue deliciously awarding him his coveted doctorate while the Public Orator at the degree ceremony admonished: "Ah! Let not excessive love of country drive to rashness, and do not resort more than is proper to alliances, stratagems, and plots!"

"I went down to the Cape thinking I will take the North," Rhodes once said. But during the Parliamentary enquiry after the fiasco of 1895, he feared that they might take his name off the map of Rhodesia. "They can't take it away from me, can they? Did you ever hear of a country's name being changed?" Today after eighty some years it is about to be changed.

Paradoxically while much of Rhodes' African legacy lies in smithereens, his Oxford legacy flourishes as never before. Indeed many of his scholars have themselves fought the world's fight on sides he would have deplored, and enlisted in causes that to him would have been anathema. In helping dismantle his African political legacy, some Rhodes Scholars have even become the Founder's laughing heirs.

However, as the beneficiaries of the thriving part of his legacy, we, for our part, are ironically now being tested in the precise terms which the Rhodes will specified. His "leadership requirement"-- the obligatory link between education and the public service and the admonition to his scholars to "esteem public duties as their highest aim"-- did not seem to be working out that way at first. In 1945, midway in the history of the scholarships, one critic wrote: "That the Rhodes Scholars have done so little except become admirable husbands and fathers shows what Rhodes really understood about the qualities required from greatness in others." Frank Aydelotte, in his 1946 book on the first forty years, also lamented that "…so few have entered government service and political life."

No longer. In the last two decades there has been a veritable explosion of Rhodes Scholars in government, both elective and appointive—Senators, Congressmen, Justices, Governors, a Speaker of the House, a Chairman of the Foreign Relations Committee, a Secretary of State, an Attorney General, an NSC adviser, a CIA director, an Army Secretary and Chief of Staff, a Librarian of Congress, numerous ambassadors, agency and commission heads, and assistant secretaries.

The electoral politics of a dozen states have been affected. The careers of Rhodes Scholars in banking, business, education, the foundations, law, journalism, science and writing have also become less and less private, and more and more public. Rhodes would have liked all that.

In the old days we were warned against taking ourselves too seriously. Perhaps we ought now to take ourselves just seriously enough to ask some probing questions. It was suggested that I should ask two or three before I sit down. Let me try.

The idea of a university harbors many societal values and, over the years, they have often been found at Oxford. Among them are civility, substantiality, and the courage to revitalize. Present or absent, these three virtues can make a decisive difference in the level and quality of our public discourse, in both our national and international life. It is here, if anywhere, that "investments in people" pay off. Let me conclude with a few words about each.

Civility. Our public discourse is increasingly shrill, acrimonious, antagonistic, and often inarticulate. Instant skepticism, automatic rigidities, and innate suspicions are the hallmarks of public life. Yet one of the merits of an education consists in resisting the impulses of nature, and demonstrating the possibility of persuasion by argument and example, rather than by intimidation and force. Despite the political scientists, we know that not all public relationships are reducible to coercion, exploitation, mathematics, and power equations.

There remain such positives as knowledge, truth, and wisdom; beauty, wit and taste; generosity, tolerance, and fairness; and life-affirming, world-affirming disinterestedness. We may differ on how to rate these virtues, but they add up to civility. Where else is contemporary society to experience them if not from those who, at some point in their lives, had the privilege of absorbing them as axiomatic?

For most of this century several dozen American Rhodes Scholars have had the chance to do so annually. Surely some of that tradition has been absorbed, like sunshine in old wine, ready to be decanted in our new plethora of public assignments, to moderate the crudities and roughness of our Hobbesian times.

Substantiality. As our senior honored guest, Professor Merriam, writes in the current Oxonian: "Oxford gave us a sense of substantiality." Compared with the pervasive provisionality all around us, substantiality reminds us that the purpose of an Oxford education was to fill ourselves out, to make ourselves complete, to focus on the bigger picture, to join that "Society for Viewing Things as a Whole." The integrative processes of an Oxford education aimed at personal cohesion, set in a sense of the past, but focusing on the future.

Substantiality is meant to supersede dilletantism, mere cleverness, the illusion of creative activity, the bland leading the bland. Substantiality is often the missing ingredient in what passes for our great debates, so undistinguished by originality, command of material, or sustained insight. Substantiality summons us to be serious about central things.

Finally there is the courage to revitalize. The West in the twentieth century has experienced a significant narrowing of choices. It is the better part of wisdom not to narrow them further. Indeed perhaps the central political problem of our time is how to enlarge and hold more middle ground both at home and abroad, extending our choices, repairing the broken dialogues, and opening new circuits of communication instead of closing them down.

On at least three continents, societies are vexed by the seemingly inexorable drift into odious national choices between the communists and the sons of bitches. The security issues and the equality issues increasingly arise on opposite sides of an almost geological fault line in the conduct of foreign policy. Everywhere there is need for broadening the base, for revitalizing the center, for breaking the flight to the extremes.

Constructive moderation is in short supply as the controversies over SALT, the Middle East, and North-South relations clearly show. While remaining faithful to our individual angles of vision, how do we collectively put more constructive synthesis into the dialectic? The courage to revitalize is another part of the Oxford experience. It urges us to help mix the cement that holds societies together, rather than collaborate in the seductive processes of national and international disintegration.

Civility, substantiality, and the courage to revitalize-- the better angels of our nature might try to retrieve these half-learned lessons from our youth and put them to work. To the degree that we do so, we will have earned our keep.

And then I suspect that neither our consciences, nor our critics, nor our wives, will begrudge us an occasional moment of sentimentality—to evoke the mystic chords of memory of that ancient stone city that packed so much beauty into so small a space. Sensitive to the half-tones of Oxford life, we reflect on the efficient secret of Oxford—those affectionate ties which, as Burke said, "…though light as air are strong as links of iron"--that lifelong bond of fellowship which Rhodes hoped the Oxford experience would infuse among us.

When I left home for Balliol in 1947, a Carleton College professor who had influenced me greatly gave me a book inscribed with the words of William Morris, Exeter, 1853. I know of no better way to close than with them:

"Fellowship is heaven,

and the lack of fellowship is hell;

Fellowship is life,

and the lack of fellowship is death;

The deeds that ye do upon the earth,

it is for fellowship's sake that ye do them;

And the life that is in it shall live on

forever."

TEARING OR MENDING?
Moderator's Remarks:
American Rhodes Scholars Reunion
Georgetown University
Washington, DC, June 12, 1993

Years ago Emerson laid down a rule that when old friends meet after a time apart they should greet each other by asking: "Has anything become clear to you since we were last together?"

Jack Justice informed me that I was mandated to moderate this opening session on its unwieldy theme: "A World Tearing Apart or a World Mending Itself?" I protested that I was now retired and too old for such an assignment. Having just left the Carnegie Endowment after twenty years, I have been reincarnated as a senior scholar at the German Historical Institute.

Jack said that was no excuse, and that perhaps some highlights gleaned from the vexatious dustbin of Anglo-Germans relations might even be an appropriate introduction for today's panel.

Having recently returned from visiting both places, I can assure you that that historically vexed relationship continues to be fragile.

An Anglo-German Preface

In a sense Anglo-German tensions, amplified by the two world wars, have been especially complicated for Oxford. Indeed those tensions are probably more moderate at Oxford than elsewhere in Britain.

A century ago Kaiser Wilhelm I actually visited Oxford. In fact he subsequently kept in touch, through his friend Professor Max Mueller, with the strong German philosophical influence at Oxford in the 1870s and 1880s. Occasionally the monarch even wired his congratulations on Oxford's boat race victories.

In the Rhodes will setting up the scholarships, Kaiser Wilhelm II was given the responsibility of appointing the German Rhodes Scholars. Amid several earlier kings of Prussia, the large portrait of Wilhelm II, wearing his red doctoral robe after his Oxford degree, still looks down, frightening students in the Examination Schools.

The Balliol College deaths in the first year of World War I included sons of both Prime Minister Asquith and German Chancellor Bethmann-Hollweg. New College chapel has its famous plaque with the inscription: "In memory of the men of this college who, coming from a foreign land, entered into the inheritance of this place and returning fought and died for their country in the war 1914-18."

Today Balliol is memorializing another German graduate, the diplomat Adam von Trott, who was hanged for his complicity in the July 20 attempt against Hitler in 1944. But those are exceptional--and very specifically Oxonian-- footnotes in a persistent and difficult history.

A more typical English attitude emerged at an afternoon tea a few years ago, also at Oxford. Searching for small talk to start the conversation, my hostess began by remarking: "Of course, Mr. Hughes, I am not an expert on foreign affairs, but, I must say, I do take such satisfaction over the continued division of Germany. Don't you?"

Such episodes regularly recur on both sides of this great divide. Recently in Bonn, I attended a lavish birthday party for a German official who, among other things, was being awarded an OBE by Queen Elizabeth. No sooner had Her Majesty's ambassador risen to present the order to the German honoree, than the German waiter dropped a huge tray laden with the dinner plates containing our main course. There was a loud crash and Henry Kissinger, sitting across from me at the head table, said: "Another disaster for Anglo-German relations."

A week later in Trier, I visited the bourgeois house of Karl Marx's parents. An Englishman ahead of us had already signed the guest book with the comment: "Too bad, Karl, it just wasn't on, was it?" (I thought of Harold Laski's response to his hecklers at Oxford when we were students there: "Leave them alone. After all, we are all followers of Marx. They in their way, I in his.")

There have been, of course, important inhibitions behind all the delicacies which have characterized the Anglo-German relationship in recent generations. Even in the late nineteenth century, the future King George V as a young man had tastes that ran to sea-going and stamp collecting, rather than the discipline of learning a foreign language. Thus in spite of all his German antecedents, he was vexed by the constant corrections of his German tutor. One day he simply put his foot down: "Der, die, or das Sommer is really very hot today. Choose which you like, Professor." By the late 1930s Foreign Minister Lord Halifax was wistfully complaining: "I often think how much easier to manage the world would have been if Herr Hitler had chanced to have been at Oxford."

And in those same years Oxford was the scene of another delicious episode, this one featuring Lord Lothian, who was then secretary to the Rhodes trust before he became ambassador to Washington. The story was told to me at a boat race dinner in the 1960s by Elvis Stahr, a Rhodes Scholar and President Kennedy's first Secretary of the Army. He had the following account of two Rhodes House banquets which he had attended in the late 1930s. The prewar German Rhodes Scholars were still in residence at the time.

At the 1937 dinner in Michaelmas term, there were three toasts: to the King, to the President of the United States, and to the Chancellor of the German Reich. Many in the room remained ostentatiously seated for the third toast. Lothian was sufficiently alarmed over this impertinence to call an urgent meeting of the Rhodes trustees, to discuss how to avoid a similar episode the following year. After an anguished discussion, the trustees found a solution. Next year they would combine the toasts to the President and the German Chancellor into a single toast to the two of them.

So at the next annual banquet in October, 1938, a month after Munich, the first toast was: "To the King" and everybody stood up. Then came the toast: "To the President of the United States and the Chancellor of the German Reich." More than half of the room remained seated, including Elvis Stahr. Whereupon the old trustee sitting next to him put his hand on his shoulder and said: "Good for you, young man! I wouldn't stand up for that Franklin D. Roosevelt either!"

Oddly enough toasts have continued to vex the postwar Anglo-German relationship. One famous occasion starred one of the Federal Republic's less distinguished postwar presidents, Herr Lubke, a former Minister of Agriculture. It fell to him to be the first German head of state to visit England since 1912. At the formal dinner at Windsor Castle, the German President rose to his feet and, facing Queen Elizabeth across the banqueting table, said: "Und now, please up-stand and join in the famous old toast: 'Upon the Queen!'"

Once in a while, however, there are attempts at magnanimity. I will close these Anglo-German reminiscences with one of them. I am thinking of former Prime Minister Harold Macmillan's visit to Washington in 1980. A splendid dinner in his honor was supposed to be followed by a question period afterwards. The famous, but aging, guest took his place on a little dais. He was resting on his cane. His eyes were closed and he was looking very inert.

The chairman said in a loud voice: "Now who has the first question for the Prime Minister?" The assembled Washingtonians were unaccustomedly silent. For his part Macmillan continued to sit with his eyes shut, looking asleep or worse.

Rather desperately, the chairman then resumed: "Well I see Tom Hughes is in the audience. He is an old Balliol man. I'm sure he has a question for the Prime Minister." Attempting to rise to the occasion, I said in a very loud voice: "Prime Minister! I have just been reading a biography of the Kaiser. It seems that in the 1870s his mother, the Princess Royal, and his grandmother, Queen Victoria, thought it would be a good idea for the young prince to study at Balliol. But Bismarck vetoed the proposal as unsuitable for a future German monarch. Query. What would have happened if the Kaiser had gone to Balliol?"

Macmillan remained motionless. Nothing stirred. There was growing apprehension in the audience. Finally the cane moved slightly. Gradually one eye opened, then the other. Suddenly the former prime minister became fully alert, responding in a firm voice: "He would have won the war!"

Varieties of Contemporary Experience.

Enough. Dave Barry, perhaps America's funniest writer these days, turned his attention recently to Miami, Florida. He described Miami as "a richly diverse cosmopolitan metropolis where people from many different cultures live and work together, while continuing to observe the traffic laws of their individual countries of origin."

Such paradoxes were apparently what worried your planning committee. In their wisdom they asked each speaker to address the topic: "Disintegration and Reintegration in a Global Society." This has been translated in your official program to read: "A World Tearing Apart, or a World Mending Itself?"

Of course, we quickly offered President Clinton another chance to come over and greet his fellow Oxonians. We thought he might want to give us some reflections on tearing-and-mending in Washington. However, he declined, saying that he was spending most of his time on non-intellectual matters these days.

By contrast, each of the intellectuals here on the stage represents a quite distinct career experience. Each has been invited to address uniting or disuniting, in terms of his or her own discipline and interest in contemporary social trends

After the initial three presentations, for fifteen minutes or so, the speakers will react to one another's comments. If all goes well, that will allow some time for individual questions from this vast audience. Each of you has been supplied with one of these very small note pads. Their size is designed to concentrate your thoughts and your questions. I say that now, so that you can plan accordingly how to reduce your own comments to questions, as succinct and pointed as possible.

Our first speaker will be A. E. Dick Howard (Virginia and Christ Church 1957). Following PPE at Oxford, Dick Howard earned his law degree from Virginia and then served as law clerk to Justice Hugo Black on the U.S. Supreme Court.

Active in public affairs, including public television, Dick was executive director of the commission that wrote Virginia's new constitution. He has been counsel or chairman of many other commissions and official bodies. Dick is widely known as an authority on constitutional law and is the author of prize winning books and articles.

When Adam and Eve left the garden, Eve reportedly turned to her companion and said: "Adam, we live in a time of transition." Much of the world has turned regularly to Dick Howard for help in constitutional transitions, from Brazil to the Philippines. Most recently he has been advising on constitutions for the Russian Republic, Hungary, Poland, Romania, the Czech Republic, and Albania.

Drawing on his experience with newly emerging democracies, he intends to comment on comparative constitutional experiences—on Western and non-Western ways of organizing societies. Professor Dick Howard.

Our second speaker is Arthur Kroeger (Alberta and Pembroke 1956). The first organizing secretary of the Rhodes Scholarship Scheme when the scholarships were set up ninety years ago was a Canadian of imperial inclinations, George Parkin. He was a fundraiser and was known in some quarters as the "bagman for the empire." It was said of him that he never got God and Oxford and the empire wholly separated.

Since then, as Tony Kenny pointed out last evening, a parade of Canadians has lent distinction both to Oxford and to Canadian public service. Our next speaker is one of the most eminent of them. He has had a long and noteworthy career as a Canadian government administrator, first serving from 1958 to1971 as a foreign service officer, followed by a stint with the Treasury Board Secretariat. Subsequently, he served as Secretary of the Ministry of State for Economic Development, and held no fewer than five deputy ministerial positions: Deputy Minister for Indian and Northern Affairs, Deputy Minister of Transport, Deputy Minister for Regional Industrial Expansion, Deputy Minister Energy, Mines, and Resources, Deputy Minister of Employment and Immigration.

Today we catch him also in transition. He has retired from government service and is now the chancellor- designate of Carleton University, Ottawa. He will reflect now on governance issues, minuses and pluses. Arthur Kroeger.

Our third speaker is Naomi Wolf (Connecticut and New College 1985).

Our founder, Cecil Rhodes, once confronted Queen Victoria, one of the leading female activists of his day, on her home turf at Windsor Castle. "And what are you engaged on at present?" asked the Queen, cheerfully. "I am doing my best to enlarge Your Majesty's dominions." Rhodes replied. When told afterwards that Rhodes was a confirmed woman- hater, Victoria responded" "Oh, I don't think that can be so. He was so very civil to me."

Of course, neither party to this encounter had the advantage that I have had of reading Naomi Wolf's best selling book, "The Beauty Myth." Had Victoria read it, she would most definitely not have been amused. Had Rhodes read it, women would probably have qualified for Rhodes scholarships on round one, at the beginning of the century.

Naomi Wolf is a Yale graduate as well as a Rhodes Scholar. In "The Beauty Myth" she teaches us that obsession with beauty is the last way that men can defend themselves against women claiming power. Her book made me aware of how culpable I have been, as part of the male minority, in perpetuating 'necessary fictions' and 'vital lies,' promoting beauty until it has become a currency system like the gold standard.

"The Beauty Myth" is a full-scale feminist manifesto indicting the plastic surgery, diet, cosmetics, and pornography industries--written by one who is proud to be known as a feminist activist.

Despite evidence to the contrary, she is in a great Oxford tradition. For example, Eleanor MacGregor from St. Hugh's, who once taught chemistry at the University of Witwatersrand in South Africa, used to have a large framed motto on her office wall which read "Don't tell them to do it. See that it is done."

Miss Wolf says: "I'm trying to seize this culture by its collar and say, "Stop! Look what you are doing!"

Naomi Wolf.

AN ANGLO-AMERICAN UPDATE
Class of 1947 Rhodes Scholars Reunion
Williams College, Williamstown, MA,
June 22, 1996.

Fellow classmates:
A few weeks ago Bruce McClellan called and announced: "You are to be toastmaster at our reunion in June." "Not again," I protested, since my life has been punctuated by similar commands in the past. "Yes, once more," he insisted. I remembered our Founder's altercation with a promising Rhodesian child: "I'll send you to Oxford, my boy." Promising Rhodesian child to Rhodes: "Oh no you won't."

I also felt a rare affinity for Henry Kissinger. At the Princeton commencement he was confronted by an irrepressible reporter who waved her microphone in front of him and pleaded with him "to say something historic." Looking at the assembled throng, Henry said, "No, no, not to such a small group."

Having succumbed—definitely for the last time--I am now reminded of an after dinner speech at St. Antony's Oxford, a few years ago. After dessert and coffee, and while the port was making its rounds at the high table, the warden turned to me and said: "Are you ready to speak now, Mr. Hughes, or shall we let them enjoy themselves a little longer?"

Actually I qualify less and less for these assignments because my Oxford connection has become increasingly obscure. They seem to know my home address when it comes to the "Campaign for Oxford," but otherwise over the years I have gradually become a non-person.

I had scarcely gone down from Balliol before they razed my first-year ground floor rooms on the quad to erect a new British-restaurant-type structure that they considered an improvement. The demolition of my digs resumed in the 1970s. This time it was the splendid Tudor Inn, just inside St. Giles Gate, Balliol's only remaining medieval structure of significance. I lived there rather grandly behind leaded windows my second year. During a recent summer vac when no one else was there, it was demolished by the scouts because they found it "powdery".

Other remaining traces of my Oxford career are also being removed. My persona itself was recently consigned to oblivion along with my lodgings. This took the form of a letter on the stationery of the warden of Rhodes House saying that the Register of Rhodes Scholars was "now quite out of date." The letter stated:

"We have drawn up a provisional entry, containing information about you. I enclose a copy of the proof of your entry. If we do not hear from you, we will assume that you have no objection to our printing the proof as it stands."

Enclosed was the biography of one Philip William Hughes (Tasmania and Wadham), ex-teacher in the Royal Australian Navy College, author of "Introduction to Calculus. 3s 3d." I haven't had the heart to correct this entry and return it for the Register. It is rather like the de-Stalinzation of Eastern Europe. It would be hard to prove that I was ever there at all, were it not for certain vivid memories.

Despite all this evidence to the contrary, I do distinctly recall spending two years at Oxford's most self-satisfied college. Indeed Balliol's renowned nineteenth century master, Benjamin Jowett, declared that his purpose in life was "to inoculate the world with Balliol." He used to advise British Viceroy-designates "Never apologize. Never explain. Get it done, and let them howl."

These words of the old master re-invigorated me when, by accident, I found myself back in England for another two years in 1969-1970, courtesy, this time, not of Cecil Rhodes but of Walter Annenberg. The circumstances were idiosyncratic, and I was the beneficiary of some comic high relief. The Nixon Administration had come to power and sent its chosen ambassador to London. As a Kennedy-Johnson holdover, I had, of course, made my plans to leave the State Department and I was waiting rather impatiently for my replacement.

Suddenly Secretary Rogers appeared in my office. "We have this new ambassador in London," he confided, "and we want you to go and help him out." I protested that they were waiting for me at Brookings. Did he know what he was doing? I had once worked for Hubert Humphrey. All to no avail. "We know all about you. You are the best solution in sight."

"Don't you think," I suggested, "that you had better clear this with the Director General of the Foreign Service? They don't like having their plumb assignments given to political appointees. They will be baffled by this one, as I confess I am." Rogers later allowed that the Director General was enthusiastic over the move. Perhaps the Foreign Service wanted my job at State.

As for me, I was reminded of that famous meeting at the Union League Club in New York in February 1917. Theodore Roosevelt was consulting his friends Elihu Root and Charles Evans Hughes. It was two months before America entered the war, but TR was eager to get into it ahead of time. He waxed eloquent about how he would volunteer and never come back; his sons also would go to France, and they too would never return. But his old enemy President Woodrow Wilson, was refusing permission for them to go. Finally, Root with his usual sagacity said: "Theodore, if you can convince Wilson that you will not come back, he will let you go."

Under rather similar circumstances, I found myself back in Britain—this time at the London embassy where Oxford kept intruding into our consciousness, often in unexpected ways. I will limit myself to a single flavorful vignette of a memorable day in embassy life in May 1970.

Glimpses from Grosvenor Square.

Our invasion of Cambodia had led the morning news, but it was not the subject of the ambassador's staff meeting. Instead the agenda items were as follows:

The Administrative section announced that President Nixon's frowning photographs, five dozen of which had arrived two weeks earlier for display in embassy offices, were to be taken down immediately and replaced by five dozen smiling photographs of the new Nixon, which had just arrived by Pan American overnight express from Washington.

Administration also noted that there were still only two signatures in the memorial book for the late Ambassador Joseph P. Kennedy. It had been on display with the Marine Guard for several weeks. Kennedy was not overly popular in Britain, and the two signers seemed to be tourists from Boston. The ambassador himself suggested: "Let's close the book and send it to the family for auld lang syne." It took some imaginative staff work to circumvent this ambassadorial instruction.

There was then a discussion of the ambassadorial garden party, scheduled for Friday. He asked how we could spend less than 20,000 pounds sterling if Princess Margaret was coming. Under the new embassy regime, the accountants had already become accustomed to adding a couple of zeroes to the previous expenditure allowances. They readily complied, seeing no way to spend less.

The security section reported that they were fully equipped to handle any American students living in England who inquired about their draft status at home. (Only twenty-two years later did we learn that Bill Clinton was already at Oxford and in need of our help.)

The cultural affairs section reported that several new words and phrases had appeared in the latest edition of the Concise Oxford Dictionary including "acid house," "ecstasy," "ghetto blaster," "leg warmer," and "street credibility." The ambassador remarked that he was not familiar with any of them.

The research section reported the retirement of the former head of the Foreign Office Research Department. Asked what was the secret of his success over a lengthy diplomatic career, he had replied: "Whatever happened, I would always say that there will be no war. I was only wrong twice."

The staff meeting then adjourned because the ambassador was hosting a lunch for Prime Minister Wilson at Winfield House. When he arrived, the PM said he had come to "inspect the refurbishments." Ignoring this attempt at joviality, the intended recipient of the remark took the PM out to the garden.

There, resuming his joviality, Wilson suddenly said: "Ambassador, it will interest you to know that the Cabinet unanimously approved the 'agrément' for your successor this morning." Thunderstruck, the Ambassador fell back rather indelicately onto a nearby garden bench. There followed a loud ambassadorial whisper in my direction: "What did he say?" I attempted to reassure. "I think the Prime Minister was joking, Ambassador. I am sure it was a joke." Agitation gradually subsided.

After lunch and the Prime Minister's departure, the ambassador's chauffeur soberly informed us that we would be returning to the embassy through a side street. We would use an auxiliary entrance, because Grosvenor Square was in turmoil.

Busloads of American students from around Britain had converged on the embassy to protest the invasion of Cambodia. The American School in London had been dismissed for the day so the sons and daughters of embassy personnel could join in the protest. By the time we reached our offices and peered out of our windows, half the London police force, mounted on horseback, billy-clubs in hand, backs to the embassy facade, were facing hundreds of milling, chanting, gesticulating young Americans.

"Is the eagle still up?" the Ambassador inquired. He looked momentarily relieved when told by Administration that the giant gilded American eagle was no longer in place, hovering over the embassy and the square. He himself had heard it was an unpopular symbol and had ordered it taken down for pigeonhole replacement and re-gilding. He had not yet decided whether it would ever be put back.

Suddenly, down below us in Grosvenor Square in front of the police, the familiar figure of my 13-year old son Evan was to be seen tossed high in the air, then caught in a blanket, and then tossed up again. Occasionally other embassy children volunteered for similar duty. But we did not know at the time that a future American President, down from Oxford for the occasion, was one of the ringleaders at the rear. Bill Clinton was already known at Oxford as the "cleverest man at Univ," just as our luncheon guest, Harold Wilson, had been a generation earlier. So, without realizing it fully at the time, we experienced Univ's two cleverest men, both of them, within a matter of a few hours, stoking controversies in two controversial settings.

Years later in Washington we were to learn that, prior to Oxford, Clinton had graduated from Georgetown where his history professor, one Carroll Quigley, had assigned the class his pioneering work on "The Anglo-American Establishment."

Now at the turn of the century, about the time Rhodes was writing his wills, Britain's foremost admiral, Jacky Fisher, announced that he was finished with going to the Continent. "The flood of Americans is so overwhelmingly nauseous and disagreeable that I will never come abroad again," he wrote. "Foreigners cannot distinguish them from English, and so I am not surprised that we are so unpopular abroad."

Unaware of such tensions, Bill Clinton and his classmates at Georgetown learned how Cecil Rhodes and Lord Milner, like King Arthur, had established a group called the Round Table. It was said to be the inner circle of front organizations like Chatham House and the Council on Foreign Relations. "I know of the operations of this network," Professor Quigley wrote, "because I was permitted in the early 1960s to examine its secret records." Just why he encouraged his star pupil to apply to go to Oxford under these circumstances has not yet been disclosed.

Quigley would have been even more alarmed had he known about a subsequent Georgetown event. In 1988 a former British ambassador, Sir Nicholas Henderson, came back to speak at a Georgetown University forum on varieties of diplomatic experience in America. He compared the terrifying expertise inside the Beltway with an "encounter out in the country several thousand miles west of here."

"I was asked to appear on a university radio program," Nicco reminisced, "and the young lady interviewer began by saying 'Sir Nicholson (sic), I must tell you that I don't know anything about your country except that there is trouble in Northern Ireland and that Princess Di is pregnant.'"

"There was a pause, and I remarked that those were clearly two very important facts. But then, overcome with curiosity, I asked whether there was nothing else whatever that she knew about Britain." "No, absolutely nothing else," she said. "We then proceeded to have a somewhat unstructured discussion, and I was happy when the subject shifted to East-West relations."

Lately, in Washington, we have had memory aids like those appearing annually in Dossier Magazine's ambassadorial biographies. Dossier's contemporary account gives us a picture of the current ambassador and the basics about him—his Oxford college of course, his languages, and his recreational pursuits. As recently as the Reagan days this magazine summarized what we might call "The Complete Dossier History of Britain" in four sentences, as follows:

"England was conquered by William of Normandy in 1066. An early military and economic power, Britain built a huge colonial empire that reached its apogee under Queen Victoria. Following World War II the nation lost or relinquished virtually all of its overseas possessions. Its current Prime Minister, Margaret Thatcher, retains a firm grip on political power." Mrs. Thatcher undoubtedly liked that sketch, hitting the highlights as it did—William of Normandy, Queen Victoria, and Mrs. Thatcher.

Even in New York City, formerly thought to be the citadel of the establishment, Anglo-American relations have begun to wane. It is true, however, that David Owen met his wife Debby at a party in Manhattan given by the venerable English Speaking Union--surely the most tangible achievement of that organization in many years.

Recently with the Labour Party back in office, some of us were reminiscing about the Labour victory of 1945. Unlike J. Edgar Hoover's personal motto "No Left Turn," the old Labour slogans that we remembered from the '40s were "Go Left! Stay Left!

Keep Left!" Today, as ex-Labourite David Owen himself would say, "The question is What's Left?"

A Non-Person Revisits Oxford

When I last took a train to Oxford there were more departure difficulties than ever at Paddington Station in London. I am sure I heard the broadcasting system announce: "This train is running ahead of schedule due to the lateness of the trains following."

The electronic information board near the platform carried a warning: "Please note that the 'Next train to Oxford' indicator is not working." A paper below added "and will probably never work again unless someone knows how to repair it."

Soon, another hand-drawn message was tacked up reading: "Passengers are requested not to join the train arriving on platform 4 as it might transpire not to be the 13.30 to Oxford." And, according to a British rail pamphlet, offered free upon request, "Intercity trains will in future be punctual if they are up to ten minutes late. Previously they were punctual if they were up to five minutes late."

I knew I was back in Oxford when I arrived at Oxford station and the graffiti across the adjoining wall read: "Karl Marx is alive and living at Balliol. Staircase XXII." And in front of the church next to the Martyrs Memorial, there was a sign which read: "A message from the Vicar: If you are tired of sin, step in." Neatly written below was the text: "But if you are not, phone Cumnor 47943."

Across the Broad from Balliol there now stands a tourist theme park called "The Oxford Story." For several pounds, moving desks whirl visitors, preferably Japanese, through centuries of architectural glory—"an informed and witty insight into the romantic past of the colleges and buildings," according to the brochure.

When I crossed over to Balliol I was surprised to see signs that read: "Closed to visitors." "No busking." "Staff only." "Strictly No Entry." Two Japanese tourists had come over from the theme park and were there at the front portal ahead of me. One had produced a camera while the other posed. I thought it was a moment of innocent and rather touching tribute from halfway around the world. Floreat domus de Balliolo.

"That'll be one pound," said the vigilant assistant porter emerging from his lodge. The Japanese looked puzzled. "Admission charge" he persisted, coming out and confronting the fare dodgers. The Asians paid their fine, set aside their camera, and scampered away.

Balliol! I know the colleges are scrambling to avoid bankruptcy. I know Mrs. Thatcher cut the subsidies in retaliation for her failure to get an honorary degree. But the idea of anyone paying to see Butterfield's pink Victorian chapel steeple is too much to comprehend. Advancing to the porter's desk, I announced that I was an old member of the college and asked whether I must also pay. " Might you possibly have an appointment with someone?" he inquired. "Yes," said I, "with the Master." "Oh, and what would you be discussing with the Master?" he asked. "I think he wants to talk about fundraising," I said. "No charge."

That night at high table the Master was entertaining the dons with the latest Thatcher story—the one about Mrs. Thatcher inviting her Cabinet to dinner at a London restaurant. The waiter deferentially approaches the prime minister, asking: "What will it be for you, Ma'am?" Mrs. Thatcher replies: "I'll have steak." The waiter inquires: "And what about the vegetables?" "They'll have steak too," she answers.

For their part the dons were claiming credit, somewhat belatedly, for discovering the latest Balliol game designed by the students against their tutors. The game consisted of deciding, over Monday morning breakfast, which large, inappropriate phrase they would all try to slip by their tutors that week. The most recent favorite had been the phrase "the last train to Vladivostok" which had somehow been woven into a number of essays at Balliol for nearly a week before it elicited any comment. I felt like suggesting a substitute, something like "the last train from Paddington," but refrained.

So Oxford remains incurably Oxford. My first-year roommate at Balliol has been translated into the Corpus Professor of Latin and normally writes commentaries on

Cicero. Last year he shared with me an unofficial draft, submitted in Latin, for the Orator's use in President Clinton's degree ceremony at the Sheldonian. While the draft ultimately was not used, it has some unforgettable lines.

It begins: "Wilhelmus Jeffersonius Airplanus Clintonensis."

It mentions: "…quondam Rhodus Scholasticus et Marijuana non-inhaliensis et ex bello Vietnamensis non conscriptione excusatus."

It alludes to: "sleazissimus in nominee 'Aqua Blanca' scandalus…cum multae bimbones."

It concludes: "…tua fama extended pro joggendo, juvando ad saxophonum et non much else."

I am willing to share the full text later on a one-to-one basis with reliable Democrats only.

George Plimpton recently ran a humor project in his magazine. You were asked to respond to the query: "What is the American state of humor today?" The hands-down winner was: "Arkansas, without a doubt." It is good to know, therefore, that while Bob Dole has publicly narrowed his post-election options to either the White House or home (presumably Russell, Kansas), by contrast Bill Clinton, if and when he is out of office, may still want to claim his third year at Oxford. He's much better than Dole at preserving his options.

Of course, Clinton could then also return to the Oxford Union. President Bush said in his 1992 campaign: "I am no Oxford debater. I didn't spend a lot of time in the Oxford Debating Society." But Clinton did. Others are also beating a path to that door where Bush feared to tread. In recent years, the Oxford Union has added conspicuously to its repertoire of notable or notorious celebrity speakers like Mother Theresa, Richard Nixon, and Kermit the Frog.

The latest was O. J. Simpson, who came on what was called "a redemptive visit" to the Union last month. He apparently left the youthful debaters mesmerized as only a fallen hero could.

Just as Richard Nixon made his first significant address at the Oxford Union after resigning from the Presidency, this was O.J.'s first significant address since his acquittal. He explained how the Bible helped him through his ordeal, particularly the Book of Job. Before his trial he had regarded the Bible as a mere book of fables. While he was in jail, however, the Bible taught him perseverance. In his Union speech, O.J. disclosed that each day, as he walked down the hallway on his way to the trial, people whispered Biblical recommendations to him as he passed: "Job 26" "Juice-Psalm 23."

Hundreds of Oxford students listened to O.J. for ninety minutes and he got a hung jury. Penelope Farthing, a psychology student, concluded: "He was too smooth, too easy going, for someone who was innocent." But Catherine Snook from St. Hilda's disagreed: "I don't know whether he's innocent, but I believe he believes he's innocent."

Denwin Jenkins, a philosophy major, said: "O.J.'s just a corrupt chess piece in a whole corrupt chess game with corrupt lawyers, corrupt media, and America's corrupt criminal justice system." Jason Puskar, an American graduate student who had been waving a placard outside that said "Murderer," decided that "O.J. came across as someone who was having too good a time. Of course, he was hardly going to stand up at the Union and say 'Hey, I'm guilty.'"

Thus does Oxford continue to educate impressionable young minds of the next generation.

For our part we emerged from Oxford half a century ago and returned to the States, like Oscar Wilde, with nothing to declare but our genius. We had admonitions running in our ears along the lines of Golda Meir's later advice: "Don't be humble; you're not that great."

Actually, in retrospect, our 1947 class has not done badly. To the federal government we supplied an attorney general who doubled as undersecretary of state; a real general; a real admiral; various ambassadors, DCMs, assistant secretaries, and Foreign Service officers; a counsel for both the Inter-American and Asian Development Banks, and a director of NIH.

We can boast several noteworthy chemists, physicists, scientists, engineers, directors of laboratories, and a distinguished surgeon. To the NGO world of foundations and think tanks we contributed a half dozen presidents and directors. To academia we supplied at least five university, college, or preparatory school presidents.

We have held hundreds of trusteeships, directorships, and honorary degrees. We even snared the presidency of the American Association of Rhodes Scholars for a while. And we produced a pride of professors--twenty or more—but I am glad to say we limited ourselves to only seven lawyers. I now call upon one of them, Frank Tatum of San Francisco, who happens also to be the one world class golfer in our group, to give the Toast to the Founder.

On one occasion, a hundred years, ago a Vice Chancellor of Oxford said: "You can't get reason out of young men, so you might as well get rhyme." That sentiment produced Victorian poet laureates like the one who was asked to compose a single couplet the invention of the telegraph and the illness of the Prince of Wales. The result then was: "Across the wires the electric message came. He is no better. He is much the same."

Fortunately we have our own, far more distinguished, poet laureate. Rhyme-less or not, our wordsmith, Bill Smith, will now read us the ode he has prepared especially for this occasion.

Our final speaker is Ed Shannon, the president of the University of Virginia. Ed is a lifelong connoisseur of Tennyson, some lines from whom seem apt for our Valedictory:

"Tho' much is taken, much abides. And tho'
We are not now that strength which in old days
Moved earth and heaven, that which we are, we are."

ABOUT THE AUTHOR

Thomas Lowe Hughes grew up in Minnesota, graduating from Carleton College in 1947. He earned post-graduate degrees from Oxford and Yale Law School. After Air Force service, he was a chief assistant on Capitol Hill for Senator Hubert Humphrey and Congressman Chester Bowles. During the Kennedy and Johnson administrations, he was Assistant Secretary of State for Intelligence and Research. In 1969-70, he was minister in the US Embassy in London. From 1971-91, he was President of the Carnegie Endowment for International Peace.